The Midnight Gate

How to Open Heaven's Door and Bring Desired Results to Your Prayers

Val Egbudiwe

ISBN: 978-1-60383-226-7

Published by:
Holy Fire Publishing
717 Old Trolley Road
Attn: Suite 6, Publishing Unit #116
Summerville, SC 29485

www.ChristianPublish.com

Printed in the United States of America and the United Kingdom

Dedication

I dedicate this book to my beloved wife, my gem, best friend and ministry supporter, Edith and my beloved daughters, Chiamaka, Chile, Neche and son, Muna. You are all precious and priceless gifts from God.

Acknowledgements

My gratitude goes first to my beloved wife, Edith whom the Holy Ghost used to confirm His leading and compel me to start writing my first book. Thank you sweetheart for all the sacrifices you make to enable me to excel in my call to serve Jesus Christ. I am indebted to my wonderful children, Chiamaka who typed the manuscript, Chileziem, Chinecherem (Neche) and Munachimsoaga for their prayers and excitement to see dad publish his first book. I am very grateful for all the support and love I have always received from all my biological brothers, sisters, numerous nephews, nieces and in-laws. I will not fail to say thank you to the Elders and members of Chapel of Revival and Miracles, the dynamic congregation God uses me to pastor in Mesquite (Dallas), Texas, USA. You are a great family. I love you all. I say a big thanks and God bless you to Apostle George and Pastor Grace Akalonu for their spiritual support and prayer cover, all my affectionate covenant brothers and friends, including Bishop Leonard Ummunna, Apostle Emanuel Duncan, Pastor Ken Straight, Pastor Charles Lincoln, Apostle (Dr.) Max and Pastor Linda Ahanonu, Apostle Reginald Carson, Prophet (Dr.) Richard Fletcher, Pastor Chryss Okonofua, Pastor O.C. Obikaram, Pastor Taiwo Ayeni, Pastor (Dr.) Joe Omeokwe, Dr. Muna Chira and Bishop Goddy Okafor. I say thank you for all your friendship and support in Ministry!

Endorsements

The Kingdom of God on earth is definitely blessed with the awesome revelation contained in this ground breaking book! This is not just a book; it is much more: a training manual suitable for use by individuals, families, small groups as well as in churches and Para church groups to pray effectively and war against the kingdom of darkness. I spent the better part of Tuesday, July 7 2009, reading through the manuscript and my heart leapt for joy because the author avoided the trap many who write on spiritual warfare fall into: the tendency to present fleshly and soulish insights to the people of God.

In this work, the multi-dimensional nature of the callings and gifts of God deposited within His servant come across so clearly. Called to be an Evangelist, Val Egbudiwe writes with the passion of one who is anointed by the Holy Spirit to set captives free and break yokes that prevent His people from possessing their possessions. As one who has pioneered a local church congregation, Chapel of Revival and Miracles, Mesquite, Texas as Pastor, Val writes with the passion of a true under shepherd of Christ who yearns to see John 10:10 fulfilled in the everyday life experience of the elect.

More importantly, Evangelist Val is a man of prayer and a vessel yielded to the Holy Spirit. Mesquite, the hitherto sleepy neighborhood of Dallas, Texas is better off today and on the way to achieving its redemptive purpose because Evangelist Val dared to hear from and believe God who called him out of the urban jungle of Africa, even the great city of Lagos to go expand His Kingdom in the community with an Indian sounding name. Like Abraham of old, Evangelist Val stepped out in faith and soaked with prayers, he has broken the ground for the gospel to flourish in the land.

Knowing the grace of God on Evangelist Val, I am excited that the Lord God has found in Him a fit and proper vessel to bring forth the awesome, biblical and intensely practical book of prayer that you have in your hands. I am excited that the Lord God has chosen this year to release the deeper dimensions and mysteries of prayer to the Kingdom oriented Church. First the Lord brought forth the epic "Victory at the Gates" through Apostle Vance Russell, my mentor who oversees Arise Ministries International in Austin, Texas. Now, the Lord has gone ahead to bring forth this ground breaking manual through Evangelist Val Egbudiwe, Founder of Val Egbudiwe World Outreach in Dallas, Texas, USA. I see these two books arming the Church of Jesus Christ with the right arsenal to plunder the gates of the enemy and recover without fail, all that were stolen from the elect.

It is with utmost joy and a great sense of responsibility that I commend this book to the Body of Christ all over the earth for diligent study and application. May it be received, read and acted upon for the greater glory of God and constant defeat of the enemy of our souls, amen!
Unto He who is the only wise God, the great Potentate, I commend this book to fulfill the assignment for which He brought it forth, amen!

May the Lord also ensure that His servant, Evangelist Val, his family and ministry are blessed from this book according to the law of seed time and harvest.

Apostle George Akalonu
International Coordinator
International Ministers Fellowship, Inc.
London, UK.

*****

The Christian book shelves are full of writings on the topic of prayer, but very few are as insightful and strategic as "The Midnight Gate" by Evangelist Val Egbudiwe. One of the greatest needs in the Body of Christ today is for the Church of Jesus Christ to rise up and pray properly. Most prayer lacks the knowledge of the will of God and cannot deliver the needed results. As Brother Valentine states, we have to use our "Prayer Gene" and utilize what God has put in us. With proper Biblical understanding, unction from the Holy Spirit and this book, we can do this and open Heaven's door to receive the results that we desire! "The Midnight Gate" is a great tool for us as followers of Jesus Christ to accomplish the mandate that is put before us. I do believe if you read and study this book it will not only revolutionize your prayer life, but revolutionize our world!

We need these strategies so as to change things in our lives, ministries and the world around us. Bowing to the will and purposes of God is only found when we pray properly and I believe this book delivers in giving us practical, relevant, insightful and out of the ordinary understanding and wisdom in the area of prayer. "The Midnight Gate" is a good "how-to manual" that Believers can use to pull down strongholds and make advances in the Kingdom of God without spending expendable time wondering and hoping if their prayers are being heard and answered. I like the way that Evangelist Val uses the Scripture to keep us focused on the task and the goal. The "Prayer Points" contained in the book are good tools to help retain and implement the principles he has conveyed. I see this book as a great resource for not only personal study but also use in small groups.

As a co-laborer with Pastor/Evangelist Egbudiwe and while serving together in Nigeria, I saw the dedication and reliance that this man of God places in the area of prayer. He not only believes in what he writes and speaks, but he has experienced the benefits of this way of living. I've seen that "keeping your prayer in God's view" is one of the keys to his success and that prayer does not have to be a leap into the dark, but a purposeful interaction with the Living God, who desires for us to succeed in the mandate that He has placed before us. I recommend this book whole-heartedly for anyone who wants to break free from a lack-luster prayer experience!

Ken Straight, Pastor
Mackinac Island Bible Church
Mackinac Island, Michigan, USA.

*****

In James Chapter 5, the Scripture tells us about Elijah who in his human nature prayed effectually and the heavens gave rain and the earth brought forth fruit. Significantly, the earth is already filled with fruits but only when the heavens allowed rain that we see manifestation. In this book 'The Midnight Gate', the author, Evangelist Val makes sincere spirited efforts for you to understand the importance of gates and how you can take advantage of them especially the midnight.

Dr. Humphrey Erumaka,
General Overseer,
Wordbase Assembly,
Lagos, Nigeria.

*****

This book, 'The Midnight Gate' is a powerful and insightful tool to be utilized by the end time Christian warriors that make up the body of Christ. It will minister to every Christian that has called out to God with a desire for a deeper and more fulfilling prayer life. Many faithful and obedient Christians have been wondering why they have not seen more answers and manifestations concerning their petitions in prayer. This book offers many insightful and revelational answers concerning those very issues. It reveals key strategies for the seasoned intercessor and the person that is just learning prayer alike. No Christian is left out of this book in any way. It meets each person right where he or she may be in their relationship with the Lord. It is written in a manner that is authoritative, yet loving, and will most certainly challenge each and every reader to get "violent in the spirit" and take back what the devil has stolen. No longer will the people of God be satisfied with letting the devil have the freedom to do whatever he pleases. The army of the Living God is ready to battle and to meet the devil and his forces at the "midnight gate" through prayer.

Evangelist Val in this book has given to the body of Christ, a powerful end time weapon and I am certain that whoever has the privilege of reading and applying it will never approach the privilege of prayer the same way. I pray blessings upon every reader in Jesus' name.

Apostle Reginald A. Carson, Senior Pastor
God's House of Miracles Church,
Grand Prairie, Texas, USA.

Foreword

Recently, the Lord revealed to me that He has released a fresh anointing and a new appreciation to the Body of Christ for prophetic intercession. He told me to expect to hear many ministers unfold deep revelation on the nature, scope and function of intercessory prayer that will make such an impact in the spirit world that we will witness irrefutable evidence of the manifestation of great breakthroughs in the natural.

The Lord said that He is taking His Church beyond the begging mentality that has marked our private prayer sessions and corporate prayer meetings. Religion has kept the Church ignorant of its rights, power and authority that God has given to us as His children. Consequently, we have been operating like the children next door asking the neighbor for a chance to pick some fruits from his tree and hoping he will say "Yes." Religion has blinded us to the truth that we have been adopted into the family of God with the same rights and privileges of son ship that Jesus enjoys and, as such, the house, the yard, the tree and all the fruits on it are ours. As a result, as long as we are walking in obedience to the Father, we are entitled to partake. The right and privilege to partake of what the Father owns are built into the authority that He has given us to decree and declare things and see them come to pass, even as Job did in Job 22:28, AMP—"You shall also decide and decree a thing, and it shall be established for you; and the light [of God's favor] shall shine upon your ways."

This is certainly a whole new way of approaching the task of intercessory prayer. It is a radical departure from tradition into an exciting experience that will bring results every time we pray. The child of God will now walk with greater confidence; intercede with pinpoint accuracy and work with God to bring things into being. You see, each of us carries the expressed image and likeness of God within us. As such, just as He created the earth by speaking things into existence, so, too, do we have that empowerment, as His children, to bring His purposes to pass in the earth with the words of our prayer.

When we engage in prophetic intercession—declarative, authoritative, Spirit-led prayer—our mouth becomes God's mouth. Since what comes out of His mouth always accomplishes what He desires and since He watches over what He proclaims to ensure a performance of the thing, it stands to reason that, in this season of a fresh, new anointing for intercession, being breathed by God over the Church, we are now being accurately aligned and greatly empowered to mount a devastating assault on the gates of hell to possess them and establish the authority of God in the earth by our prayers.

This new book—THE MIDNIGHT GATE—written by Evangelist Val Egbudiwe, is a manifestation of the prophetic shift that God has made in His Church, as it pertains to intercessory prayer. It is a virtual manual that takes the reader through a step by step process that will remove the darkness of ignorance from his mind by shedding the light of fresh revelation upon the screen of his spirit. The child of God who will put these instructions into practice will lead a more successful life both spiritually and naturally.

I decree that this book will touch lives across the earth and that it will be used by God to liberate His people from bondage of begging prayers and the frustration of unanswered petitions. It will also be used as an instrument in God's hands to help raise a new breed of prayer warriors. Moreover, I declare that, by virtue of Evangelist Val writing this book under the unction of Holy Spirit by virtue of a download of the mind of God, He is not only an Evangelist but also a Prophet, endued with an apostolic authority.

PROPHET VAL, YOU BELONG WITH EAGLES, SO KEEP ON SOARING AND DON'T STOP UNTIL YOU GET TO THE TOP!

Apostle Emanuel Vivian Duncan
Divine Destiny Worship Centre
Trinidad W.I.

Table of Contents

Introduction

Prayer is not supposed to be a frustrating spiritual activity because God is very willing to answer your prayers. He promised this in His word.

> ***"Ask, and it will be given to you; seek, and you will find; knock, and it will be opened to you."***
> ***(Matthew 7:7, NKJV)***

Maybe right now your prayer is not getting the results you desire. You are not the only one who suffers; many things in your life, your marriage, job, finances and spiritual life could all be adversely affected. You can agree with me that the way you have prayed up till this moment will not be enough for what you are experiencing in the hands of the devil.

It is very unfortunate that today, irrespective of all the evil experiences and happenings of the time, many people and "Christians" are still living under the illusive deception of religious traditions. They claim to be saved, born-again, tongue-speaking children of God only to go to church on Sundays, sing and dance to praise and worship songs, still maintain their sinful old habits and spend little or no time praying. In fact, most times, the prayer is left for the Pastor to do with the assumption that all will be well as long as the Pastor does the praying. Well, I want to inform you that all will not be well. In fact, all has never been well under these circumstances.

As a man of God, I had discovered that I did not get my desired results in prayers every time neither did members of the congregation that I pastor. I started a search to what have been missing. I read and studied many books on prayer. My discovery was that the prayer techniques enumerated in many books required a lot of work to follow. What then can be done? I was led to search the Scriptures to find out what made the prayers of the men and women of God in the Bible to work. I discovered two major stunning patterns:

- Your TIME of prayer is pertinent.
- The WORDS of your prayer are critical.

Jesus Christ is the role model for all Christians. When His disciples asked Him to teach them how to pray, He started this very important teaching by saying – "…when you pray, say..."

Take note of the words **'when'** and **'say'**.

> ***Now it came to pass, as He was praying in a certain place, when He ceased, that one of His disciples said to Him, "Lord, teach us to pray, as John also taught his disciples." So He said to them, "When you pray, say:***
>
> ***(Luke 11:1-2, NKJV)***

When you pray and what you say are very important in getting the door of heaven opened and releasing the desired results to you. A critical search of the Scriptures will reveal to you that most of the miracles and great prayers of the Bible had a lot to do with the kind of words used as well as timing.

- Paul and Silas in Philippi prison had to wait until midnight before engaging in their earth quaking prayers.
- God's judgment against Egypt was executed at midnight.

There are no special people that God answers their prayers. You have everything it takes to get the desired results to your prayer as long as you are a born-again believer. All you need to do is to know when to pray, what to say and some other important simple but effective prayer principles very easy to follow which I have enumerated for your guide in this book.

I was challenged by my discovery as a Pastor that most of the churchgoers of today never see the manifestation of many miracles and blessings they claim and prophecies they receive in the church. These people are missing something. I discovered they are not using the right prayer timing. In this book you will discover that the midnight is a critical time to pray. I call it a 'gate' because it marks the end of the night and the beginning of a new day. Take advantage of this revelation. The midnight gate is a strategic entry location into a new day, week, month, or year. You need to stand in this important spiritual strategic location and release your spiritual arsenals through prayers against the devil. You need to turn your battle against the forces of hell at the midnight gate in other to open heaven's door and get the desired answers to your prayers. You need to possess the gates!

When you ponder and closely monitor all what is going on today, you will understand that Satan has shifted and repositioned himself in the spirit realm. He is adopting uncommon ways of onslaught to get at God's children. You too must shift and reposition yourself. The midnight gate prayer is the key! You need to totally realign yourself in order to be effective in launching prayerful counter attacks on this spiritual level. Adopting the midnight gate key, your prayers will become pointed and sure, targeting directly at the point where they will cause the most damage to the evil forces working against you thus releasing your blessings. Your time has come to possess the gates.

I have included in the last chapter of this book, a 21-Day Midnight Gate prayers. Please do try my suggested prayers and send me feedback with your praise reports.

What you have in your hands will challenge you and revolutionalize your prayer life.

You are a prayer eagle!

Chapter 1

You Have a Prayer Gene

God created mankind with everything needed to receive the blessings of life. God is willing to answer your prayers and grant you the desires of your heart. He clearly stated this fact in the Bible:

> ***"Call to Me, and I will answer you, and show you great and mighty things, which you do not know"***
> ***(Jeremiah 33:3, NKJV)***

When you call Him, He answers. This means you have what it takes to call Him! Many Christians are going through ups and downs in life today because they are yet to come to terms with the truth that God has deposited a special 'gene' which they require to call upon Him and get answers. You may have read books on prayers, listened to sermons about prayers but you still feel frustrated because your prayers do not produce your desired results. This makes you feel that you are not part of God's anointed prayer eagles. Friend! This is a lie from the pit of hell. Your problem is that something needs to be activated in you. Something needs to come to life!

You are a prayer warrior!

You are a prayer eagle!

God created you to bring to pass His purposes on earth and make things happen when you pray. What you need to do is to activate your prayer gene.

Dictionary.com defines gene as:

"A hereditary that occupies a specific location on a chromosome, determines a particular characteristic in an organism by directing the formation of a specific protein…"

Based on this definition, I describe the prayer gene as a divine deposit placed in you by God during creation to enable you have an effective communication with Him to bring about the manifestations of your heart desires according to His will and purposes. This divine deposit needs to be activated.

Several times in your life you feel you are on the other side of the river of life watching the opposite side where other people are celebrating the feast of life with joy and happiness. That may be where you are now. My prayer for you is that as you read this book. God will stir up something that will propel you to assume your rightful position in the club of God's prayer eagles.

In the gospel of John Chapter 5, the Bible talks about folks who gathered at the pool of Bethesda waiting for an angel to stir the pool for them to jump in and receive healing. A particular man was there who has been sick for 38 years.

> ***"Now a certain man was there who had an infirmity thirty-eight years. When Jesus saw him lying there and knew that he already had been in that condition a long time, He said to him, "do you want to be made well?" The sick man answered Him, "Sir, I have no man to put me into the pool when the water is stirred up; but while I***

am coming, another steps down before me."
(John 5: 5-7. NKJV)

This man that has been sick for 38years lying at this pool must have heard several shouts of rejoicing by those who made it into the pool and got healed. Several folks there must have been stepped, trampled upon and pushed down by others on their ways to struggle to get a dip into the healing pool. This particular man says he does not have a man while a man was standing in front of him. Although the pool of water has not been stirred but the man had no idea what manner of person was asking him **"...Do you want to be well?"** With the presence of Jesus there, he does not have need of the pool nor a man to put him into it. Many people are yet to make use of the divine deposit (prayer gene) in them and bring about the miracles they so much crave for in their lives.

You may be by the pool today. You may be going from one man or woman of God to another seeking for prayers. May be you feel you don't have "any man" like the man by the pool of Bethesda, who could pray one of those fire brand prayers to bring about the manifestation of your miracle. Are you on the other side of the river watching others in their joyous splendor rejoicing and celebrating the feasts of their lives? I want to tell you today that you can set up a bridge across that river to take you to the other side so that you can join the celebration and feast of life. All you need is to put your prayer gene into use.

Activate your prayer gene!

The Lord has empowered you from creation to build that bridge and change your life forever. Quit going from one church to another, from one revival meeting to another, looking for an anointed man or woman of God to lay hands on you. How many times have hands been laid upon you? What about all those prophecies you have received? You still do not notice any significant change. The reason is simple - you need to activate your prayer gene. God is waiting on you to act. He wants you to do it yourself because He gave you all you require. That is why He said.

"Call to me and I will answer….."
(Jeremiah 33:3 NKJV)

You have all it takes. You have the ability. It is located in you. All you need is to stir it up. Take a decision today and say to yourself.

"I have what it takes"

"I don't need any other person to pray for me."

"God will answer me"

Friend, I am not saying it is wrong for others to pray for you. I do pray for people. I pray for members of the congregation which I pastor. I pray for my family and loved ones. All I am saying is that you have all it takes to pray for yourself as much as that person whom you are asking to pray for you. Do not depend on someone else to pray before God can answer.

You may be saying now that you have been praying but how come you don't see the accomplishment of those petitions? The answer is simple. Many Christians do not know how to pray to get heaven to rain them with positive results. This is why I have written this book. I need to put into your hands some profound revelations that will challenge you and usher you into that realm of miraculous and supernatural outpouring that accompany the lives of God's praying eagles.

God says:

> ***"You ask and do not receive, because you ask amiss..."*** ***(James 4:3 NKJV)***

Many God's children need to know when and how to ask and receive. However, the foremost thing is to activate the divine deposit in you needed for effective prayers. You are a born intercessor, a prayer warrior, a prayer eagle. No one prays better than you because you've got what they got. There is something God has put in you that need to come alive; it needs to wake up. This is the prayer gene!

In 1996 while in Lagos, Nigeria, Africa, my daughter who was at that time, less than two years of age fell very sick at about 3.00a.m. She was having severe vomiting and diarrhea. There was no Emergency Clinics in Lagos, Nigeria then and if we had to take her to a private hospital at that time of the morning, we would have been required to make a huge financial deposit before the physician could attend to her. My wife and I did not have the money at that time. The only option we had was prayer so that God will divinely heal her. There was no way we could reach our Pastor at that time of the morning as GSM mobile phones were not yet in use in Nigeria then. I pondered over what to do as the baby wriggled and cried in pain. Suddenly, the Lord spoke to my heart – "you can pray for her. You have all it takes to pray!" I was still a 'baby Christian' although I have been called into Ministry. As soon as I heard the voice of God, my wife and I knelt down beside the bed and placed our hands on the baby just as the word of God in Mark 16:18 came to my heart:

> ***"…. They will lay hands on the sick, and they will recover. "*** ***(Mark 16: 18. NKJV)***

As we prayed fervently in spirit and in understanding, I suddenly felt a hot glow of fire all over my palms laid on my baby. Before we could finish praying, the baby who had been restless and crying for the past one hour, slept and never woke up until 9.00a.m. When she woke up, the diarrhea and vomiting had stopped. We never took her to any hospital or any Pastor to pray for her. I then realized that I have something in me for I only need to open my mouth and pray. Friend, you have the special gene for prayers. Activate your prayer gene.

Prayer Points.

Prayers to activate your prayer gene and kindle the fire upon your altar of prayers.

Confession:

Personalize these Scriptures and confess them aloud before you begin to pray.

- ***I can do all things through Christ who strengthens me.*** ***(Philippians 4: 13 NKJV)***
- ***And the fire on the altar shall be kept burning on it; it shall not be put out…*** ***(Leviticus 6:12a NKJV)***

1. O Lord, cleanse all the contaminated parts of my life and wash away all my sins with the blood of Jesus Christ in Jesus name.
2. O Lord, send the purging fire of the Holy Ghost upon me now and let the lust of flesh in my life die in Jesus name.
3. Let the seed of prayer divinely deposited in me be kindled by the flame of the Holy Spirit and let it blaze upon the altar of my heart in Jesus name.
4. I wake up from any spiritual slumber and I put on the whole armor of God in Jesus name.
5. Holy Spirit, ignite my prayer life and let my spirit-man become divine fire in Jesus name.

Chapter 2

Keep Your Prayers in God's View.

A very important principle for getting heaven's door open and bringing desired answers to your prayers is to bow to the will and purpose of God. You must be sincere and frank as regards the motives hidden in your heart. Remember God knows and sees your heart.

> ***… O Lord of Hosts, You who test the righteous, And see the mind and heart***
>
> ***(Jeremiah 20:12a, NKJV)***

You must not pray amiss or else your prayer will not bring the desired results.

> ***You ask and do not receive because you ask amiss, that you may spend it on your pleasures.***
>
> ***(James 4:3, NKJV)***

Selfishness is the mother of wrong motives in prayer. You must give up selfishness if you must have your prayers answered. Selfishness is all about yourself and not God. This means that selfishness is related to rebellion. God does not approve of rebellion. Remember, rebellion cost Saul his kingship.

> ***"…For rebellion is as the sin of witchcraft, and stubbornness is as iniquity and idolatry. Because you have rejected the word of the LORD, He also***

has rejected you from being King"

(1 Samuel 15:23, NKJV)

You must learn humility, obedience and complete surrender which is the opposite of rebellion. Jesus adopted obedience and complete surrender when He prayed in the garden of Gethsemane.

> ***"Father, if it is Your will, take this cup away from Me, nevertheless not My will, but Yours be done"***
>
> ***(Luke 22:42, NKJV)***

The garden of Gethsemane was the second garden which constitutes the 'gate' of destiny of the second Adam. The make-up of this garden which is purely submissive prayer is completely different from those of the first garden which was the Garden of Eden. It was a very beautiful garden with all necessary provisions for Adam, the occupant.

"The LORD God planted a garden eastward in Eden, and there He put the man whom He had formed"

(Genesis 2:8, NKJV)

A companion was even made available for him in the person of Eve. They were blessed by God and given ruler ship over all that God created.

> ***Then God blessed them, and God said to them, 'Be fruitful and multiply; fill the earth and subdue it; have dominion over the fish of the sea, over the birds of the air, and over every living thing that moves on the earth' (Genesis 1:28, NKJV)***

Adam was doing pretty well in the garden to the extent that he was having fellowship with God until Satan struck with disaster. Satan came with lies and temptation. Adam fell to the temptation. Adam never used the weapon that Jesus, the second Adam used in the second garden. That is the weapon of a well positioned prayer, a prayer kept in God's view. No wonder he fell to the temptation of Satan. Temptation leads to sin and sin takes you away from God's presence and as a result, away from his purpose for your life. Whatsoever that will wade you off God's will for your life begins with temptation. Your ability to overcome temptation depends on the quality of your prayer before and not after the temptation. No wonder Jesus warned:

> ***"…Pray that you may not enter into temptation"***
> ***(Luke 22:40, NKJV)***

Man through Adam lost so much in the Garden of Eden. But God, who is full of compassion and mercy, was set to restore what was lost in the first garden.

> ***The Lord is gracious and full of compassion, slow to anger and great in mercy***
> ***(Psalm 145:8, NKJV)***

He put together another garden in Gethsemane with the second Adam as His only begotten Son, Jesus Christ. Jesus Christ had a mandate to recover the dominion, power and glory lost by the first Adam. He was able to carry out this assignment successfully because while in this garden he positioned his prayer for God's attention. He kept His prayer in God's view.

"…not My will, but Yours be done."

(Luke 22:42b, NKJV)

Jesus was in great agony. He was tempted to abandon the assignment set before Him. But he was quick to realize that it was not about how he feels but the will of God for Him. If you need to swing open heaven's door and bring desired answers to your prayers, no matter what you are praying about, you need to first discover what the will of God is concerning that situation and have your prayers positioned accordingly. God's will on any issue in your life is always in conformity with His plan and purpose for your life. Irrespective of the fact that Jesus felt like giving up the assignment before him, He had a perfect understanding and knowledge of God's purpose for sending Him to the earth.

> ***…just as the Son of Man did not come to be served, but to serve and give his life a ransom for many.***
>
> ***(Matthew 20:28, NKJV)***

Equipped with the knowledge and purpose of His coming, He was able to keep His prayer in God's view. In John chapter 10 verse 10, Jesus re-iterated:

> ***"…I have come that they may have life, and that they may have it more abundantly."***
>
> ***(John 10:10, NKJV)***

God's will in sending Jesus to the earth was to give His life as ransom, pay the penalty for man's sins and secure abundant life for humanity. Sin in the human race had its origin in Adam and

Eve. The sin of the first Adam and his companion, Eve made them corrupt in nature and this involved the whole human race. The effect of sin is that whoever is living in sin has chosen a life independent of the Creator. Sin is not in conformity with the will of God and this was what Jesus Christ came to the earth to deal with. God needed to address the issue of sin once and for all. The primary and most important purpose for which Jesus Christ, the Son of God came to the earth was to save mankind from sin.

"...He will save His people from their sins."
(Matthew 1:21b, NKJV)

Jesus Christ understood that his distinguished mission and purpose was to settle the question of sin. Every other miracle He did was also done by the prophets. Because He realized this simple purpose, He was able to position His prayers for God's attention.

"...not my will but Yours be done."

What is God's will concerning your prayer request? Is it in line with God's purpose for your life?

> Your life has a purpose in God's agenda. Everything has a purpose. Anything without a purpose is ineffective. Until purpose is discovered, life has no meaning.

When you pray according to the purpose of God for your life, you keep your prayer in God's view. A lot of people today do not know the purpose for their prayer issues. Be careful about ignorance. Ignorance is a very destructive force in getting answers to your prayer issues. It is very dangerous to be ignorant of God's will for you because it leads you to spending so many hours in prayer and never know why you prayed. Many people have said to me that what they do not know cannot destroy them. They say to me that God knows all things and will grant them whatsoever He feels necessary. Sure! I believe that God knows all things for the Bible says so.

> ***…God is greater than our heart, and knows all things.*** ***(1 John 3:20, NKJV)***

However, even though God knows all things, He still requires that you pray. He says you should ask. You need to ask.

> ***"Ask, and it will be given to you…"***
> ***(Matthew 7:7, NKJV)***

I need to address the issue of ignorance by letting you know that it is not an excuse that you are ignorant of a thing because what you do not know can kill you! Whosoever drinks a cup of hydrochloric acid will be poisoned even though the cup may be labeled 'soda'

> ***If a person sins, and commits any of these things which are forbidden to be done by the commandments of the LORD, though He does not know it, yet He is guilty and shall bear his iniquity*** ***(Leviticus 5:17, NJKV)***

Whenever you pray against the will of God for you, you pay dearly for this because such a prayer will not be positioned effectively for God's attention and effective answer from God's throne room. You need to have a sound knowledge of

God's purpose for your life in other to pray according to His will concerning issues of your life. The only person that is in the rightful position to give a profound knowledge of the purpose of anything is the manufacturer. The creator is the only competent one who knows the purpose of its creature. If you ask a refrigerator why it was manufactured, you will not get a response but ask the manufacturer and you will be told of the need to cool, freeze and preserve food substances. The same is applicable to mankind. God is the Almighty Creator of mankind and as a result is the only one fit enough and capable to give a revelation of His purposes for your life. God has already spoken about the purpose of your creation but you have not been able to discover it. This is why Proverbs chapter 25 verse 2 says:

> ***It is the glory of God to conceal a matter, But the honor of kings is to search out a matter.***
> ***(Proverbs 25:2, NKJV)***

Everything God has said concerning the purpose of your life is contained in secret containers on the pages of scriptures. You need to make efforts on continual and persistent basis to search out the purpose for your life. To discover the purpose for your life, you need to study and meditate on the Bible daily because your whole life depends on it.

> ***"You search the Scriptures, for in them you think you have eternal life, and these are they which testify of Me." (John 5:39, NKJV)***

> ***"This Book of the Law shall not depart from your mouth, but you may observe it day and night that you may observe to do according to all that is***

> ***written in it. For then you will make your way prosperous, and then you will have good success."***
>
> ***(Joshua 1:8, NKJV)***

With the Word of God in the Bible as your basic foundation, pray until you discover His purpose for your life.

> ***"Pray without ceasing"***
>
> ***(1 Thessalonians 5:17, NKJV)***

The Word of God will unfold great knowledge and revelations concerning your life.

> ***"For the word of God is living and powerful, and sharper than any two-edged sword, piercing even to the division of soul and spirit, and of joints and marrow, and is a discoverer of the thought and intents of the heart"***
>
> ***(Hebrews 4:12, NKJV)***

Prayer Points

Prayers to receive a revelation of God's purpose for you.

Confession:
Personalize these Scriptures and confess them aloud before you pray.

- *"For I know the thought that I think towards you, says the LORD, thoughts of peace and not of evil, to give you a future and a hope."*
  (Jeremiah 29:11, NKJV)

- *"Before I formed you in the womb, I knew you; before you were born I sanctified you; I ordained you a prophet to the nations."*
  (Jeremiah 1:5, NKJV)

- *...and the sheep hear his voice; and He calls his own sheep by name and leads them; and the sheep follows him, for they know his voice.*
  (John 10:3, NKJV)

- *He reveals deep and secret things; He knows what is in the darkness, and light dwells with Him.*
  (Daniel 2:22, NKJV)

1. O LORD, if I have abandoned your purpose for my life, have mercy on me, forgive me and show me the right way to go in the name of Jesus Christ.

2. Let every idol present in my heart that is contrary to God's purpose for my life melt away by the fire of the Holy Spirit in Jesus name.

3. I stand against all agents of the devil and demonic powers working to cause me to derail from God's purposes for my life in Jesus name.

4. O LORD, deliver me from spiritual ignorance in Jesus name.

5. Holy Spirit, open my eyes of understanding. Help me to see and walk on the paths God has ordained for my life in Jesus name.

Chapter 3

Spiritual Violence

For your prayers to be effective and open the door of heaven bringing desired answers, you have to be spiritually violent. The problems that people experience always take place spiritually before they are seen physically. In view of this, it is important to learn at this point that spiritual problems cannot be stopped physically using ordinary weapons hence the Bible says our weapons of warfare are not carnal.

> ***"For the weapons of our warfare are not carnal but mighty in God for pulling down strongholds, casting down arguments and every high thing that exalts itself against the knowledge of God, bringing every thought into captivity to the obedience of Christ" (2 Corinthians 10:4, NKJV)***

Beloved, we are in the days of spiritual conflict between the devil and God's children. This is warfare and every war is fought with violence. Time is running out for Satan and he is launching devastating onslaughts against mankind. The televisions, newspapers, radios, and internet are all full of stories of demonic violence against the human race. News of terrorists attacks; bombings, earthquakes, wildfires, flooding, untimely deaths, hurricanes and the likes are in commonplace these days. Life is no longer safe everywhere! Isaiah, the prophet of God warned about impending darkness on earth.

> ***"For behold, the darkness shall cover the earth, and deep darkness the people,…"***
>
> ***(Isaiah 60:2, NKJV)***

The prophet Isaiah calls it 'deep' darkness. In the King James Version of the Holy Bible, it was referred to as 'gross' darkness. Gross stands for total, complete, extreme, dense, and heavy darkness. In other words, this is the kind of darkness that can be felt. Darkness is synonymous with evil. It denotes a great satanic move on the face of the earth. This darkness is already here.

* There are economic and financial woes all over the world.

* People kill and maim their loved ones without remorse.

* Teenagers and Youths pick up guns and waste the lives of innocent students in schools and colleges.

* Suicide and suicide attempts are common incidents these days.

* There are high incidents of armed robbery and kidnapping.

* Incidents of hired assassins are common even inside the churches.

The health sector is not left out as the devil has released legions of ailments and diseases some of which are incurable. Time has come for a more determined violent combat in prayers against the devil to curb his end-time onslaughts against mankind. This is a very important way to get the heavens door opened and bring quick desired answers to prayers. God reciprocates to spiritually violent prayers against the devil His enemy who is responsible for all the woes experienced by mankind today.

The Bible noted these profound truths:

> ***"He cast on them the fierceness of His anger, wrath, indignation, and trouble, by sending angels of destruction among them."***
>
> ***(Psalm 78:49, NKJV)***

> ***"Pour out Your wrath on the nations that do not know You, and on the kingdoms that do not call on Your name."***
>
> ***(Psalm 79:6, NKJV)***

In continued efforts to pour his demonic onslaughts on God's children, Satan has moved into the churches to cause God's people to derail so he could afflict them. Satan is not afraid of the churches because they are filled with bunches of 'cold believers'. Many Christians inside the churches today have lost their hedges of protection from satanic attacks for they are neither hot nor cold.

> ***"…you are neither cold nor hot. So then, because you are lukewarm, and neither cold nor hot, I will vomit you out of my mouth"***
>
> ***(Revelation 3:15,16, NKJV)***

Beloved, Satan does not love you! He is responsible for your problems and he is not ready to give you a break except you choose to get hot and fight back with spiritual violence. Satan has stolen from you, killed your dreams and visions and destroyed many good things that ought to come your way. Jesus said:

> ***"The thief does not come except to steal, and to kill, and to destroy..."*** ***(John 10:10, NKJV)***

A thief, killer, and destroyer come with violence and weapons and you don't fight back with passivity and empty hands. You got to be spiritually violent!

> ***And from the days of John the Baptist until now, the kingdom of heaven suffers violence, and the violent takes it by force.*** ***(Matthew 11:12, NKJV)***

You need to take your stolen blessings back from the devil and this requires a violent counter attack.

I told you earlier on that any manifestation on earth, first of all takes place in the heavenlies. It is important at this point to bring to your knowledge that there are three heavens.

> ***"I know a man in Christ who fourteen years ago—whether in the body I do not know, God knows—such a one was caught up to the third heaven."***
> ***(2 Corinthians 12:2, NKJV)***

Apostle Paul, in this great epistle to the people of Corinth, talks about the third heaven.

The MacArthur Study Bible explains the three heavens in this way:

- The first heaven is the earth's atmosphere (Gen. 8:2; Deut. 11:11; 1 King. 8:35)

- The second is interplanetary and interstellar space (Gen. 15:5; Ps. 8:3; Is. 13:10) and

- The third is the abode of God (1 King. 8:30; 2 Chr. 30:27; Ps. 123:1)

I want to bring to you a profound revelation. The second heaven is the headquarters of the devil! Everything that comes to you from God passes through the second heaven and anything such as petitions, supplications going from you to God also crosses the second heaven. The second heaven is therefore like an immigration post or spiritual border with demonic border patrols and immigration officers. It is in this zone that most strongmen of the devil in charge of communities, towns, and families operate. I strongly believe that it was at this point that the answer to Daniel's prayer was intercepted by the prince of the kingdom of Persia, a demonic strongman in charge of that kingdom on behalf of Satan.

> ***Then he said to me, "Do not fear, Daniel, for from the first day that you set your heart to understand, and to humble yourself before your God, your words were heard; and I have come because of your words. But the prince of Persia withstood me twenty-one days…"*** ***(Daniel 10:12,13a, NKJV)***

Daniel prayed for 21 days. His prayer was heard in Heaven but opposing powers also heard Daniel's prayers and took conscious steps to stop him from receiving his positive answer. What did these opposing powers do? They sent one of their demonic borders patrol officers in the second heaven to intercept the answer. Daniel's continued violent prayer bombardments necessitated a heavenly spiritual reinforcement that brought angel Michael into the scene and released his blessings. Your prayer ought to be spiritually violent enough to bombard through the second heaven to bring down the answer.

Elisha was a man of God in the Bible who exhibited a violent nature in his prayers. When He was surrounded by the Syrian soldiers, He violently prayed them into blindness.

> ***So when the Syrians came down to him, Elisha prayed to the LORD and said 'strike this people, I pray, with blindness' and He struck them with blindness according to the word of Elisha.***
>
> ***(2 Kings 6:18, NKJV)***

A great Assyrian army equipped with horses and chariots and weapons of satanic violence came over against Elisha. They surrounded the city. However, Elisha is a man of God who has a double portion of anointing. He knew how to get the door of heaven opened and unleash God's wrath against his enemies. He chose to engage in spiritual violence as He prayed.

> ***"...LORD...strike this people, I pray with blindness,"***

Did God honor Elisha's violent prayer? The answer is yes.

> ***...and He struck them with blindness according to the word of Elisha. (emphasis, mine)***

Satan has his weapons of violence. The most common which are spiritually coded with all manner of afflictions against mankind are the demonic arrows.

> ***For look! The wicked bend their bow, they make ready their arrow on the string, that they may shoot secretly at the upright in heart***
>
> ***(Psalm 11:2, NKJV)***

God who is aware of all the devices of the devil provided you with incredible "Believers' weapons of Spiritual Violence" for your prayers to unleash attack at Satan. Below are some of them as contained in the Scriptures.

* The name of Jesus Christ:

  Therefore God also has highly exalted Him and given Him the name which is above every name, that at the name of Jesus every knee should bow, of those in heaven, and of those on earth, and of those under the earth…"

  (Philippians 2:9-19, NKJV)

  "If you ask anything in My name, I will do it"

  (John 14:14, NKJV)

* The Blood of Jesus:

  And they overcame him by the blood of the Lamb… ***(Revelation 12:11, NKJV)***

* The fishers and hunters (Babylonian soldiers doing God's judgment work):

  "Behold I will send for many fishermen" says the LORD "and they shall fish them; and afterward I will send for many hunters, and they shall hunt them from every mountain and every hill, and out of the holes of the rocks…"

  (Jeremiah 16:16, NKJV)

* Angels of destruction:

He cast on them the fierceness of His anger, wrath, indignation, and trouble, by sending angels of destruction among them.

(Psalms 78:49, NKJV)

* Fire and Brimstone:

"Then the LORD rained brimstone and fire on Sodom and Gomorrah from the LORD out of heavens" (Genesis 19:24, NKJV)
Elijah answered and said to them, 'If I am a man of God, let fire come down from heaven and consume you and your fifty men' And the fire of God came down from heaven and consumed him and his fifty (2 Kings 1:12, NKJV)

* The Sword:

"...I will slay the last of them with the sword."

(Amos 9:1, NKJV)

"Though they go into captivity before their enemies, from there I will command the sword, and it shall slay them" (Amos 9:4, NKJV)

Prayer Points

Seven sample violent prayers against the devil that troubles your life.

Confession:

Personalize these Scriptures and confess them aloud before you pray.

- ***And the God of peace will crush Satan under your feet shortly.*** ***(Romans 16:20, NKJV)***

- ***"Let the saints be joyful in glory; let them sing aloud on their beds. Let the high praises of God be in their mouth, and a two-edged sword in their hand, to execute vengeance on the peoples; to bind their kings with chains, and their nobles with fetters of iron"*** ***(Psalm 149:5-8, NKJV)***

- ***Plead my cause, O LORD, with those who strive with me; fight against those who fight against me. Take hold of shield and buckler, and stand up for my help. Also draw out the spear, and stop those who pursue me. Say to my soul, 'I am your salvation.' Let them be like chaff before the wind, and let the angel of the LORD chase them.*** ***(Psalm 35:1-3,5,NKJV)***

"No one can enter a strongman's house and plunder his goods, unless He first binds the strongman. And then he will plunder his goods" ***(Mark 3:27, NKJV)***

1. Every curse, satanic pronouncements and jinxes issued by occultists, witches, wizards, rulers of darkness and local wickedness against my life and destiny, I break you by the blood of Jesus Christ, in the name of Jesus.

2. By the power in the mighty name of Jesus Christ, let every remote control and demonic satellites set up against me, receive the fire and brimstones of God and be burned to ashes in Jesus name.

3. I call down God's fire, thunder, lightning and tempest upon all satanic observers of the progress of my life in Jesus name.

4. O LORD, reorganize my body system, organs, vessels, and veins to reject all satanic arrows in Jesus name.

5. I use the power in the blood of Jesus Christ to cleanse my organs and systems of all satanic foods and drinks I have taken from childhood and in my dreams in Jesus name.

6. Let the angels of God arise and block the path of the satanic enemies of my God ordained destiny in Jesus name.

7. O God, send the heavenly hosts, the fishers and hunters to dig into the foundation of my life and excavate any evil deposits in Jesus name.

Chapter 4

Persistence Is Not Repetition

Jesus told the parable of a persistent friend in the gospel of Luke to show one of the most powerful spiritual prayer secrets to open the door of heaven.

> ***And He said to them, "Which of you shall have a friend, and go to him at midnight and say to him, 'Friend, lend me three loaves; for a friend of mine has come to me on his journey, and I have nothing to set before him'; and he will answer from within and say, 'Do not trouble me; the door is now shut, and my children are with me in bed; I cannot rise and give to you'? I say to you, though he will not rise and give to him because he is his friend, yet because of his persistence he will rise and give him as many as he needs" (Luke 11:5-8, NKJV)***

The parable contains a powerful and effective key to bringing desired answers to prayers. It tells us that the friend who came by midnight was able to get what he needed from his friend because of his persistence and not even as a result of the relationship existing between the two. Whenever you pray and make supplications to God, you need God to grant you a miracle. God wants to grant you that miracle accompanying your well positioned prayer. But you need to know an important fact: "Miracles accompany the prayers of those who are willing to persistently wait for it." When you want the door of heaven opened with answer to your prayer, you must be persistent in making your requests known to God.

The issue of persistent prayers is somewhat controversial within the church circles today. It is a generally accepted fact that you should not repeat prayers.

> ***"And when you pray, do not use vain repetitions as the heathen do. For they think that they will be heard for their many words." (Matthew 6:7, NKJV)***

Beloved, I pray that God will open your spiritual eyes and you will see some profound truths. Let us take a look at the prayer said by Jesus at the Garden of Gethsemane.

> ***"He went a little farther and fell on His face, and prayed, saying, 'O My Father, if it is possible, let this cup pass from Me; nevertheless, not as I will, but as You will.' Then He came to the disciples and found them sleeping, and said to Peter, 'What! Could you not watch with Me one hour? Watch and pray, lest you enter into temptation.***
>
> ***The spirit indeed is willing, but the flesh is weak.' Again, a second time, He went away and prayed, saying, 'O My Father, if this cup cannot pass away from Me unless I drink it, Your will be done.' And He came and found them asleep again, for their eyes were heavy. So He left them, went away again, and prayed the third time, saying the same words" (Matthew 26:39-44, NKJV)***

'Saying the same words!'

As Jesus prayed in the garden, He went intermittently to check on His disciples only to find them continually asleep. Each time, He will go back to continue His prayer, "saying the same words." Do you term this repetition? If you do, it then means that it is a contradiction to Jesus' own words in Matthew 6:7. This is not a contradiction because Jesus was not indulging in vain repetitive kind of prayer but rather He was persistent. Vain repetitive prayers have a characteristic which is to be seen of men but this was not the intention of Jesus. He was engaged in persistent prayer which is a great lesson to you in getting the door of heaven opened to your prayers.

Persistence in prayer is not repetition.

Elijah was persistent in his prayer that there should be rain in Israel. He persistently prayed for seven times before his servant could see a cloud of gathering rain.

> ***So Ahab went up to eat and drink. And Elijah went up to the top of Carmel; then he bowed down on the ground, and put his face between his knees, and said to his servant, 'Go up now, look toward the sea.' So he went up and looked, and said, 'There is nothing.' And seven times he said, 'Go again.' Then it came to pass the seventh time, that he said, 'There is a cloud, as small as a man's hand, rising out of the sea!' So he said, 'Go up, say to Ahab, 'Prepare your chariot, and go down before the rain stops you.' (1 Kings 18:42-44, NKJV)***

Some people may not believe that what Elijah did was persistent prayers for seven times. But a look at the book of James confirms that Elijah was actually praying these seven times. His prayer had to be persistent to open the door of heaven and bring an answer that both initiated and ended a three and a half years of drought.

> ***Elijah was a man with a nature like ours, and he prayed earnestly that it would not rain; and it did not rain on the land for three years and six months.***

And he prayed again, and the heaven gave rain, and the earth produced its fruit.
(James 5:17-18, NKJV)

Elijah did not use any prayer method that you cannot use. Remember James says "Elijah was a man with a nature like ours…" He was simply applying the key of persistence to open the door of heaven. This key is available to you! Remember it was a three years and six months of drought. This type of issue does not require an ordinary religious type of prayer. There is need for spiritual persistence. It is very pertinent to note that those issues in your life that seem spoilt, difficult and impossible can experience dramatic and miraculous changes if you can be persistent in your prayers. Once you start praying, continue persistently until the Holy Ghost either asks you to change to another prayer or to stop. There may be lots of unpleasant issues in your life that require more prayer persistently to take care of.

Be careful because you can stop praying too soon!

The story of Joash the king by the death bedside of Elisha should be an eye opener to you. Joash needed some prophetic revelations from the man of God who is about to die. Elisha prophetically revealed to him a great mystery about the defeat of their enemy, the Syrians. Elisha told him that He must strike the Syrians till they are destroyed. Let us look at what transpired in this mysterious and prophetic dialogue.

And Elisha said to him, 'Take a bow and some arrows.' So he took himself a bow and some arrows. Then he said to the king of Israel, 'Put your hand on the bow.' So he put his hand on it, and Elisha put his hands on the king's hands. And he said, 'Open the east window'; and he opened it. Then Elisha said, 'Shoot'; and he shot. And he said, 'The arrow of the LORD's deliverance and

the arrow of deliverance from Syria; for you must strike the Syrians at Aphek till you have destroyed them.' Then he said, 'Take the arrows'; so he took them. And he said to the king of Israel, 'Strike the ground'; so he struck three times, and stopped. And the man of God was angry with him, and said, 'You should have struck five or six times; then you would have struck Syria till you had destroyed it! But now you will strike Syria only three times.'
(2 Kings 13:15-19, NKJV)

There are circumstances in your life orchestrated by the devil that require you to strike the devil persistently with prayers until they are dealt with.

Some people may tell you that if you are persistent in your prayers, it is an evidence of lack of faith. Quite the contrary! Your persistent prayer is rather evidence that you have faith that your answer will come. A persistent praying person is one who holds firmly to the desired purpose not minding obstacles, delays and setbacks. Several times, peoples' blessings and desired miracles elude them because they are not consistently persistent. Whenever you position your prayers for God's attention and violently present your requests persistently using some other keys I will talk about in subsequent chapters, the door of heaven swings open and God issues a response. However, as the answer to your prayer passes the second heaven, the satanic princes at the border may intercept them, bringing delays. This is the time many people give up thinking that God has refused them. You need persistence at this time to bring about what I call 'divine angelic intervention' to release your desired response from heaven. This was the case with Daniel in Daniel chapter 10. Daniel's request was granted right from the first day he presented his petition. But the angel delegated with Daniel's answer from heaven was intercepted by one of the satanic border patrols—the prince of Persia. It took a 21 days persistent prayer by Daniel to activate a divine angelic intervention which eventually resulted in the manifestation of the answers to Daniel's request.

Persistent prayer sets in motion a divine environment that radiates a quick manifestation of spiritual power. Power belongs to those that choose persistence in prayers. Remember Jesus promised his disciples power before He left.

> ***"But you shall receive power when the Holy Spirit has come upon you…"*** ***(Acts 1:8a, NJKV)***

This promise of power was not actualized immediately until the disciples persistently waited for it in one accord and this brought about a sudden divine manifestation of power! Alleluia!

Who says persistence does not secure God's attention? The devil will always want you to stop at the first attempt in prayer. This was the case of a man called Bartimaeus. If he had stopped at the first attempt to call on Jesus, may be his miracle would have eluded him. But despite the oppositions he had with people shouting him down, he persisted in making the same appeal until He got Jesus to stand still.

> ***And when he heard that it was Jesus of Nazareth, he began to cry out and say, 'Jesus, Son of David, have mercy on me!' Then many warned him to be quiet; but he cried out all the more, 'Son of David, have mercy on me!' So Jesus stood still and commanded him to be called. Then they called the blind man, saying to him, 'Be of good cheer. Rise, He is calling you.'*** ***Mark 10:47-49, NKJV)***

Do not give up on that petition. Pray persistently until heaven's door swings open for you.

Chapter 5

What Time is it?

Timing is a very critical factor in getting the door of heaven opened with prayers. The lives of people are controlled by the clock especially in developed countries. People manage their clocks and set alarms to wake them up at appropriate times to meet up with the events of the day. But when it comes to praying, people feel it does not matter when they pray. Your time of prayer is important. Having read this book up to this page, I am convinced you want to know the truth. You need to get the door of heaven opened and your prayers receive the desired results you expect. The time you pray has a lot to do with the results you get!

I have said earlier in this book that all the activities that have brought pain to your life are the results of the supernatural onslaughts of the devil. These satanic attacks take place at a particular time and the effects manifest later. The activities of the devil that have devastating effect on man, take place in the night. These activities bring pain that cause you to cry. No wonder the Bible says:

> ***"...Weeping may endure for a night, But joy comes in the morning." (Psalm 30:5b, NKJV)***

There is a time of transition. That is a time that separates the night from the day. This is midnight. Midnight is a very critical time because it is a time of both good and evil spiritual activities. The word 'midnight' was mentioned at least fourteen times in the Bible. God Himself brought to the knowledge of mankind the significance of midnight by operating at that time.

> ***Then Moses said, "Thus says the LORD: 'About midnight I will go out into the midst of Egypt; and all the firstborn in the land of Egypt shall die, from the firstborn of Pharaoh who sits on his throne, even to the firstborn of the female servant who is behind the handmill, and all the firstborn of the animals" (Exodus 11:4-5, NKJV)***

Midnight is a gate.

I will discuss more on the 'gate' in subsequent chapter. It is a time of huge and immense destruction and calamity. Midnight is a time of judgment, evil or righteous, when decrees can be passed on a whole community, family, or individuals. You could see from the scripture above that God, the Father demonstrated the significance of midnight by waiting till that time to carry out His righteous judgment against the people of a wicked nation. Egypt experienced the wrath and indignation of God through the deaths of the firstborns of man and beast in the land. At what time did this happen? Midnight. You need to turn the battle of your life against the devil by praying at midnight. You need to do this because the door of heaven shall open for your desired results.

> **"A regular midnight prayer with violent and persistent bombardments against the forces of hell gets the door of heaven opened with incredible desired results"**

Most people are very vulnerable to the attacks of the devil at midnight. It is an hour when the evil one, the enemies of mankind lay siege against humanity. You can also take advantage of this and launch your attacks on the devil. You need to stand up against the devil at the midnight hours.

Midnight is a time of exchange for Satan. Destinies, fortunes, and blessings are exchanged for sorrows, pains, and curses at the midnight hour. Remember the story of the prostitutes in the book of 1 Kings where King Solomon showed great wisdom.

> ***"Then it happened, the third day after I had given birth, that this woman also gave birth. And we were together; no one was with us in the house, except the two of us in the house. And this woman's son died in the night, because she lay on him. So she arose in the middle of the night and took my son from my side, while your maidservant slept, and laid him in her bosom, and laid her dead child in my bosom. And when I rose in the morning to nurse my son, there he was, dead. But when I had examined him in the morning, indeed, he was not my son whom I had borne."***
>
> ***(1 Kings 3:18-21, NKJV)***

Midnight is the time of battle. Many people have missed so much because they do not understand the mystery of the midnight hour. One of the mothers in the story above lost her baby and exchanged him for another at midnight when her colleague slept. You need to be awake and fire prayers at midnight to stop all forms of satanic exchanges in your life. The mysterious evil happenings you experience in your life are hatched during the midnight hours, the day only wakes up to manifest them. All the demonic activities that oppress your marriage, your job, your finances and business are hatched during the midnight hours. They are only experienced during the day as the demonic messengers bring them to manifestation.

> ***"In a moment they die, in the middle of the night; The people are shaken and pass away; The***

mighty are taken away without a hand."
(Job 34:20, KJV)

The Scripture in Job chapter 34 verse 20 talks about the great calamity that befalls mankind at midnight. It is a time of trouble when even the mighty are attacked without a human hand. In other words, it is a time of spiritual attack. Some of these attacks result in deaths.

I counseled a sister in Nigeria who was experiencing continual witchcraft attack every night. She wakes up every morning with marks on her body after some fights in her dream the previous night. According to her, between the hours of 12 midnight and 3:00am, she will always have a dream where people are chasing her with bows, arrows, and guns. Sometimes, different kinds of animals such as cats, dogs, and wild species will be running after her in her dreams. At the end of every encounter she will awake to discover that the attack took place between the same hours of midnight. This experience continued for several months and she lost her lucrative job at a bank and developed an ailment that could not be diagnosed at the hospital. It is important to note that this sister is a born again Christian. According to her, her pastor had prayed for her, many brethren and church intercessors had prayed for her. She also prays before going to bed. However, all these prayers could not produce the desired result. The trouble which this lady was going through was pitiful. It became a sorrowful and fearful period for her each time midnight approaches and she always could not help but find herself sleeping before midnight. There are troubles at midnight beloved and you need to wake up to the challenges because sleep will cause you to lose your God-ordained destiny to Satan.

"… but while men slept, his enemy came and sowed tares among the wheat and went his way."
(Matthew 13:25, NKJV)

As I listened to this lady during the counseling session, the Holy Ghost asked me to tell her to engage in 'midnight fire prayers' for 21 days with fasting. I wrote some prayer points from scriptures and equipped her with some of the weapons of spiritual violent prayers to engage the enemy at the midnight gate. With all determination, she obediently, with great precision, commenced the prayers. Ten days into this spiritual exercise, the dreams stopped and before the end of the 21 days, a new generation bank in Nigeria offered her a job with a salary bigger than what she earned in her previous job. The undiagnosed sickness disappeared. Alleluia!!! This is God in action.

Midnight is a time that you can launch a devastating confrontation against your enemies and gets a positive desired result thereby recovering all that the enemies stole from you.

Samson was a man in the Bible that took advantage of the midnight hour to obtain victory against his enemies. Even though Samson was careless with his life as he exhibited so much weakness with people of the opposite sex, but God honored him with victory when he adopted the strategy of a midnight onslaught against his enemies' camp.

> ***"When the Gazites were told, "Samson has come here!" they surrounded the place and lay in wait for him all night at the gate of the city. They were quiet all night, saying, "In the morning, when it is daylight, we will kill him." And Samson lay low till midnight; then he arose at midnight, took hold of the doors of the gate of the city and the two gateposts, pulled them up, bar and all, put them on his shoulders, and carried them to the top of the hill that faces Hebron." (Judges 16:2-3, NKJV)***

Samson was delivered from the siege that was laid for him by awaking at midnight. You can be delivered with victory against you enemies if you can adopt the midnight prayer strategy. The event that followed the arrest and imprisonment of Paul and Silas is another landmark event that reveals a profound truth about praying at midnight.

> ***"But at midnight Paul and Silas were praying and singing hymns to God, and the prisoners were listening to them. Suddenly there was a great earthquake, so that the foundations of the prison were shaken; and immediately all the doors were opened and everyone's chains were loosed."***
>
> ***(Acts 16:25-26, NKJV)***

During the course of their mission to Philippi, Paul and Silas encountered a lady possessed with a spirit of divination. Paul, under the great anointing of the Holy Ghost, delivered the lady of the demonic spirit. You agree with me that this deliverance was of immense benefit to the girl and glorious to God. However, the action got them into trouble. They were arrested, beaten, and commanded to be thrown into prison. Instructions were given to the jailer to keep then securely and this made the jailer to move Paul and Silas to the inner part of the prison, the dungeon, and chained their feet in the stocks. Paul who has mastered the great strategy to get heaven's door opened and receive desired results in prayer waited for the right time to knock on heaven's door.

...But at midnight Paul and Silas were praying...

They waited until midnight before launching their prayer attack. It was not just ordinary regular prayers we see these days that do not produce results but rather frustration. They were engaged in violent prayers for the Bible says that other prisoners heard them. Violent prayers are not said under your breath and in low tones but with powerful aggressive crescendo as it is always accompanied with weapons of spiritual violence. Their prayer was so powerful that the door of heaven swung open and a host from heaven was spiritually released to bring about a massive earthquake that shook the foundations of the prison.

"A violent and persistent prayer said during the midnight hours is capable of shaking the foundations of any satanic misdeed in your life and bring about a release from demonic bondage"

The midnight prayers of Paul and Silas caused the doors of the prison to be opened and they regained their freedom. Another aftermath of the prayer was the salvation of an entire family.

What time is it? It is midnight! You need to respond to the devils attack at a time you can get at him. Heaven will back you up. The arsenals of heaven will be released to you. Wait for the devil at the midnight gate. Midnight prayers bring about desired results. Prayers said at the midnight gate must be violent, persistent and spiced with all the necessary ingredients of effective praying in other to replace failures with success and bring about destruction of foundational problems plaguing your life that are not visible in the physical. The midnight hour can also be an incredible time to offer the sacrifice of thanksgiving unto God to bring about His righteous judgments over your enemies.

> ***"At midnight I will rise to give thanks to You, Because of Your righteous judgments."***
>
> ***(Psalm 119:62, NKJV)***

Chapter 6

What Do I Say?

What you say during the time of prayer is very crucial in obtaining the desires of your heart. Many people have missed God's blessings and ended up in frustration after long periods of praying simply because they are saying the wrong things each time they approach the throne of God in prayers. Remember what the Bible says:

> ***"You ask and do not receive, because you ask amiss…" (James 4:3A, NKJV)***

Having seen Jesus pray with tremendous positive results following, the disciples came to Him and requested that He thought them how to pray. Does it mean that the disciples of Jesus were not praying? No! Just that they were probably not getting the desired results.

> ***"Now it came to pass, as He was praying in a certain place, when He ceased, that one of His disciples said to Him, "Lord, teach us to pray…"***
> ***(Luke 11:1, NKJV)***

Jesus Christ responded to this request with this sentence:

> ***"…When you pray, say:" (Luke 11:2, NKJV)***

This means that what you say when you pray is very critical to the answer you get. What do you say when you pray? What you say must be in agreement with the mind of God. You may ask me, "How do I know the mind of God?" The mind of God is the Word of God. God's Word is His integrity. God and His Word are inseparable. The Word of God is God!

> ***"In the beginning was the Word, and the Word was with God, and the Word was God."***
> ***(John 1:1, NKJV)***

What you say during prayer time is a very important factor in getting the door of heaven opened and bringing your desired answers. Once you have decided what to pray about, find out what God says about that and put it into your prayer words. How do you accomplish this? By studying and meditating on the Word of God. As you study the Word of God, you commit key scriptures to memory. Remember, every scripture is very important for all scriptures are given by the Holy Spirit inspiration.

> ***"All Scripture is given by inspiration of God, and is profitable for doctrine, for reproof, for correction, for instruction in righteousness, that the man of God may be complete, thoroughly equipped for every good work."*** ***(2 Timothy 3:16:17, NKJV)***

Having found the relevant scriptures, you then turn them into prayer points. I define a prayer point as "the word of God modified into a 'spiritual arsenal' for firing the camp of the enemies with persistent violence to produce devastating victory against the enemies".

If you learn how to turn scriptures into prayer points, you have achieved an incredible spiritual skill pertinent for your prayers to open the doors of heaven and obtain your desired answers.

For your prayer points to be sharp, aggressive and attract desired answers, you must have a good understanding of the scriptures. This is where the Holy Spirit is needed. You need Him to give you revelation of the truth of God's Word as contained in the Scriptures.

"...For the Spirit searches all things, yes, the deep things of God." (1 Corinthians 2:10, NKJV)

"...For the Holy Spirit will teach you in that very hour what you ought to say." (Luke 12:12, NKJV)

You must end all your prayer points in the name of Jesus.

"And whatever you ask in My name, that I will do, that the Father may be glorified in the Son. If you ask anything in My name, I will do it."
(John 14:13-14, NKJV)

It is a very necessary and important requirement that all prayers addressed to God must absolutely be made in the name of Jesus Christ. No other name has been approved by God to bring about the desired answers to our prayers. Not even the name of Mary, an Angel, a Prophet, or Saint could be substituted for the name of Jesus Christ.

The name of Jesus Christ is higher than any other name.

"Wherefore God also hath highly exalted him, and given him a name which is above every name: That at the name of Jesus every knee should bow, of things in heaven, and things in earth, and things under the earth; And that every tongue should confess that Jesus Christ is Lord, to the glory of God the Father." Philippians 2:9-11, KJV)

Chapter 7

Deal with the Obstacles

I have been confronted by believers many times concerning the frustrations they encounter in life despite their commitment to Christ and dedication in service to their churches. These people pay their tithes, give good offerings to support the work of God, sow seeds and live good Christian lives yet continue to battle with life's problems. They have been involved in various prayer programs, hands have been laid upon them, prophecies have gone forth concerning them and all these have not taken them to any where further than where they are in life.

I do not say I have the recipe that could bring a solution to the problems you face today. But I want to bring to your knowledge, some vital issues that have hindered many people which need to be dealt with before you can really be positioned to attain your full potentials in life. These are obstacles to your prayers. For your prayers to open the door of heaven and bring about your desired result, you got to deal with these obstacles. You may feel frustrated thinking that God has failed you and you are planning to quit serving and worshipping God. Beloved, God has not failed you. Thank God you are still reading this book. God says in His word:

> ***"The poor and needy seek water, but there is none, their tongues fail for thirst. I, the LORD, will hear them; I, the God of Israel, will not forsake them." (Isaiah 41:17, NKJV)***

God is still going to move on your behalf as the door of heaven opens for you. You need to apply these profound truths revealed in this book. Most of all, obstacles need to be dealt with. I am not talking about common hindrances you have read about in other prayer books such as unforgiveness, unconfessed sin, improper marital relationships etc. I am talking about obstacles that are most of the time hidden from people but still hinder their prayers.

The obstacles in your life are summarily put together in what I call 'foundational blockages'. Foundational blockages are issues in your life, most of which you may not know their origins but they block and hinder your prayers preventing them from producing the desired results. My prayer is that God will open your spiritual eyes and bring revelations to you concerning issues you need to deal with if the door of heaven must open to get the desired answer concerning that particular issue in your life. Your life is like a building. Any building with a faulty foundation is adversely affected by changes in weather. But one built on a solid foundation withstands all manner of harsh climate. Even Jesus Christ acknowledges this fact when He said:

> ***"He is like a man building a house, who dug deep and laid the foundation on the rock. And when the flood arose, the stream beat vehemently against that house, and could not shake it, for it was founded on the rock. But he who heard and did nothing is like a man who built a house on the earth without a foundation, against which the stream beat vehemently; and immediately it fell. And the ruin of that house was great."***
>
> ***(Luke 6:48-49, NKJV)***

There are tremendous 'streams' of satanic attacks beating vehemently on your life today. The foundation of your life may need repairs to withstand these attacks. This could be the reason why you seem to be going through problems that defy solution and if you would deal with these foundational problems you will get out of the present imbroglio fast.

Everyone has a past which dates back to the time of your parents and ancestors. Yes! You may be born again today but were your parents and ancestors born again? Some worshipped idols, others belonged to occult societies. They set up foundations upon which your life rests on today. There is a controversy among some believers concerning foundational problems. Some believe that they cannot be negatively affected by foundational problems because of what the Bible says in 2 Corinthians:

> ***"Therefore, if anyone is in Christ, he is a new creation; old things have passed away; behold, all things have become new."***
>
> ***(2 Corinthians 5:17, NKJV)***

I strongly believe in the Word of God as contained in the above scripture. Before you became born again you lived in alienation from God. This is exactly what the scripture means by old things. As a born again Christian, the old period of separation from God has passed away because the spirit has been born again of God. However, when you became born again, where you given a new flesh-life to replace the old one? The answer is no. When an HIV-AIDS infected person becomes born again, the disease will not disappear because the person has become born-again. God can heal the person, of course, but this healing doesn't come just because the person got saved. So it is with the foundations of your life as established by your ancestors. The consequences of the damage that has been in the past are still there. If your ancestors were occult priests, princes, and princesses of idols, then the building of your life has been erected on a faulty foundation of idolatry and you got to prayerfully deal with it. The Bible says:

"If the foundations are destroyed, what can the righteous do?" (Psalm 11:3, NKJV)

The foundation of your life determines the kind of advancement you experience just like the strength of a house foundation dictates the kind of structure that can be built upon it.

Foundational problems are represented by altars. You need to deal with altars to actualize your movement to prominence and significance in life as you pray to open the door of heaven. An altar is a place of sacrifice, worship and communion. It is a place of contact with any deity that is being worshipped. God divinely instituted an altar Himself because; there is an altar before the throne of God in Heaven.

"Then the sixth angel sounded: And I heard a voice from the four horns of the golden altar which is before God" (Revelation 9:13, NKJV)

Satan has created his own version of altars. These are evil and demonic altars, which make up the foundations of peoples' lives. These altars need to be dealt with.

Gideon is a man in the Bible who is recognized in Heaven as a 'mighty man of valor'.

And the Angel of the LORD appeared to him, and said to him, "The LORD is with you, you mighty man of valor!" (Judges 6:12, NKJV)

On earth, Gideon was living in fear, he was poor and impoverished. He was hiding from the Midianites whom he was created to deliver Israel from.

"Now the Angel of the LORD came and sat under the terebinth tree which was in Ophrah, which belonged to Joash the Abiezrite, while his son

Gideon threshed wheat in the winepress, in order to hide it from the Midianites"

(Judges 6:11, NKJV)

Then the LORD turned to him and said, "Go in this might of yours, and you shall save Israel from the hand of the Midianites. Have I not sent you?"

(Judges 6:14, NKJV)

Gideon was sent by God on a journey of deliverance to the people of Israel from the hands of their oppressors, the Midianites, but he had to deal with an obstacle that has hindered him for a long time. This was his father's altar. It was an altar built by his father for Baal, a false god introduced into Israel by one of her kings. Even though Gideon was a man known in Heaven to be full of boldness, bravery, and courage, he attested to the fact that he was the least in his father's house and his family was poor. What was responsible for all these earthly calamities? Altar of course!

"And he said unto him, Oh my Lord, wherewith shall I save Israel? behold, my family is poor in Manasseh, and I am the least in my father's house" ***(Judges 6:15, KJV)***

How you see yourself on earth today might be different from how heaven knows you. It is your responsibility to deal with altars in opposition to your prayers, so as to get the door of heaven open and bring about desired answers to your prayers. God is instructing you today just like He instructed Gideon:

"... tear down the altar of Baal that your father has, and cut down the wooden image that is beside it..." ***(Judges 6:25, NKJV)***

This was a direct and precise instruction from God to Gideon. Why was God so concerned about this? This is because without dealing with this foundational problem, Gideon's journey towards prominence and significance will end in defeat, failure, and disgrace. God instructed Gideon to replace the evil altar of Baal with an altar of God.

> ***"...and build an altar to the LORD your God on top of this rock in the proper arrangement, and take the second bull and offer a burnt sacrifice with the wood of the image which you shall cut down."*** ***(Judges 6:26, NKJV)***

It was very necessary and important to replace the evil altar with the altar of God. This is because an altar offers spiritual covering over an area where it is located. Also the type of altar existing in an area determines the kind of spirits that control the locality and the people living therein. Gideon had to tear down the altar of Baal because the Spirit of God is needed in his location to bring about the divine purpose of God for his life and that of his people. This was why men of God in the Bible such as Noah, Abram, Moses, David, Elijah, and a host of others built altars for the LORD at different times and in different locations.

Many problems ranging from financial, health, marital to even spiritual growth in your life that has resisted your prayers could be traced to evil altars that are foundational in your life. They are satanic obstacles working against you and hindering your prayers. You need to deal with them. So many people today are walking around but remotely controlled by hidden altars in the foundations of their lives. They live in developed countries where there are abundant opportunities but have nothing to show. They work like elephants but eat like ants. They are like preys in the hands of the devil to fulfill his ministry of stealing, killing, and destroying. God wants to set you free and this was why He asked me to write this book.

Follow the footsteps of Gideon!!!

You may be wondering in your heart now why these altars still have negative effects despite the fact that the Bible says that Jesus Christ took away the handwriting of the devil against us through His death on the cross.

> ***having wiped out the handwriting of requirement that was against us, which was contrary to us. And He has taken it out of the way, having nailed it to the cross. (Colossians 2:14, NKJV)***

Yes Jesus Christ took away the handwriting of the devil against you when He went to the cross but you need to discover how to make this work of redemption work for you. This is because, Jesus Christ died for all but only those that receive Him are given the power to become children of God.

> ***But as many as received Him, to them He gave the right to become children of God...***
>
> ***(John 1:12, NKJV)***

Well, these altars still have negative effects on you as a Christian because of divine fundamental rule of dedication which have been in operation even before you were created. The "Rule of Dedication" is a fundamental process whereby something is set apart for the worship of God, a spirit being or deity. God guards jealously anything that is dedicated to Him. The same thing goes for Satan. Satan closely monitors anything dedicated to him irrespective of how long ago the dedication took place, ensuring that such thing does not escape from his grasp. This could be the reason why you are still not in your God-ordained position. You got to deal with the obstacles. I want to show you a profound truth about the workings of the fundamental rule of dedication. In 1 Chronicles 18:11, King David dedicated some items to the Lord in Jerusalem.

"King David also dedicated these to the LORD, along with the silver and gold that he had brought…" (1 Chronicles 18:11, NKJV)

Several hundreds of years later, the king of the Chaldeans, Belshazzar desecrated theses articles dedicated to God and paid dearly for the costly mistake.

"…Belshazzar gave the command to bring the gold and silver vessels which his father Nebuchadnezzar had taken from the temple which had been in Jerusalem, that the king and his lords, his wives, and his concubines might drink from them. Then they brought the gold vessels that had been taken from the temple of the house of God which had been in Jerusalem; and the king and his lords, his wives, and his concubines drank from them. They drank wine, and praised the gods of gold and s ilver, bronze and iron, wood and stone." (Daniel 5:2-4, NKJV)

The late father of King Belshazzar (whose name means 'Bel, protect the King'), Nebuchadnezzar took the vessels dedicated to God several years before his son's reign and over two decades after Nebuchadnezzar's death, Belshazzar defiled the vessels dedicated to God. What was the consequence? In the same hour, the King saw a hand writing mysteries on the wall and at the same time, his body mechanism began to trouble him.

In the same hour the fingers of a man's hand appeared and wrote opposite the lampstand on the plaster of the wall of the king's palace; and the king saw the part of the hand that wrote. Then the king's countenance changed, and his thoughts troubled him, so that the joints of his hips were

loosened and his knees knocked against each other. (Daniel 5:5-6, NKJV)

The interpretation of the handwriting on the wall was given by Daniel.

> ***"And this is the inscription that was written: MENE, MENE, TEKEL, UPHARSIN. This is the interpretation of each word. MENE: God has numbered your kingdom, and finished it; TEKEK: You have been weighed in the balances, and found wanting; PERES: Your kingdom has been divided, and given to the Medes and Persians."***
>
> ***(Daniel 5:25-28, NKJV)***

Belshazzar has no knowledge of the dedication of these vessels to God, but He paid dearly for his action. In the same way, many people who have become Christians today but were similarly dedicated to satanic altars, though they have no idea about it, are being hindered by this. You got to deal with it! It is also important to note at this point that the condition of your heart could help these foundational altars to prosper in your life. Your heart is a spiritual altar for sacrifices unto your God. If your heart is filled with lust, pride, anger, envy, fear, hatred, and all manner of evil thoughts and activities, you are bringing the doors of your life open and letting in the devil to take control. Many Christians today have their hearts filled with all these evils. They may be praise and worship leaders, speaking in tongues and church leaders but their prayers will be hindered until these obstacles are dealt with.

Prayer Points

Prayers to deal with obstacles to your prayers

Scripture Meditation:

Study and meditate on ***1 Kings 13: 1-5; Psalms 11:3*** Personalize these Scriptures and confess them aloud before you pray:

> ***"For there is no sorcery against Jacob, Nor any divination against Israel. It now must be said of Jacob And of Israel, 'Oh, what God has done!'***
> ***(Numbers 23:23, NKJV)***

> ***Christ has redeemed us from the curse of the law, having become a curse for us (for it is written, "Cursed is everyone who hangs on a tree"), that the blessing of Abraham might come upon the Gentiles in Christ Jesus, that we might receive the promise of the Spirit through faith.***
> ***(Galatians 3:13-14, NKJV)***

1. I renounce any evil dedication placed upon my life and I command all demons associated with such dedication to leave by fire now, in Jesus name.

2. I break and loose myself from every inherited bondage or evil covenant in Jesus name.
3. I decree paralysis to all fundamental strongmen attached to my life in Jesus name.
4. O Lord, send Your axe of fire to the foundation of my life and destroy all evil plantings in Jesus name.

5. I withdraw any part of my body, my blood, my pictures, image or anything representing me from any evil altar in Jesus name.
6. Let the thunder of God break down every evil foundation of my life and let God rebuild a new one on Jesus Christ, the Rock in Jesus name.
7. I dismantle every territorial evil altar ministering against me and I command every evil priest ministering at the altar to receive immediate judgment of fire in Jesus name.

Chapter 8

Ingredients Needed

You may be gearing up to go into spiritual battle at this juncture. However, it is very important for you to note that the battle against the devil at the midnight gate requires some ingredients. These are necessary if you must achieve your desired results. The first and foremost thing every Christian needs, to succeed in prayers at the midnight gate is brokenness. Apostle Paul was a man that showed tremendous success in prayer at the midnight gate. Remember his incredible victory with Silas in a Philippi prison; (Acts 16). What was his secret? He used the powerful ingredient pertinent in getting heaven's door opened. He was completely broken and in total surrender to the Lordship of Jesus Christ.

> ***"I have been crucified with Christ; it is no longer I who live, but Christ lives in me; and the life which I now live in the flesh I live by faith in the Son of God, who loved me and gave Himself for me."***
>
> ***(Galatians 2:20, NKJV)***

The great Apostle Paul was dead in Christ. To prevail in prayers at the midnight gate, requires no less because you are going against violent, destructive and rebellious spirits. A small bit of disobedience and rebellion to God is all that Satan needs to find in your life as this could open you up to a disastrous demonic counter-attack. You are able to get the door of Heaven opened for desired answers to your prayers at the midnight gate using the right ingredients. Many Christians need desired answers and success in their prayers but do not use the necessary ingredients. If you are walking in total surrender to the Lordship of Jesus Christ, then you must be obedient to God's command as contained in the Word of God. Your way of life as a Christian and your life affects the fervency of your prayer in opening the door of heaven. Having a right relationship with Jesus Christ and continually seeking His good pleasure, places you in the right position to get the door of heaven opened as you pray. In other words, keep His commandments!

> ***"And whatever we ask we receive from Him, because we keep His commandments and do those things that are pleasing in His sight."***
> ***(1 John 3:22, NKJV)***

Repentance is of paramount importance in securing the desired answers to your prayers. Forsake sin! Confess and repent of your sins. God wants to answer you.

> ***"If My people who are called by My name will humble themselves, and pray and seek My face, and turn from their wicked ways, then I will hear from heaven, and will forgive their sin and heal their land." (2 Chronicles 7:14, NKJV)***

Sin keeps prayers from being answered. You must therefore use the very important ingredient of total and prompt repentance. Anything that represent sin such as anger, lust, immorality, bad temper, harsh words, all can come between you and God and frustrate your prayers at the midnight gate. Sin grieves the Holy Ghost! Confess your sins, repent of them, then go into prayers using the midnight gate approach. There is no sin, He would not forgive, if you confess, repent, and forsake them with your whole heart. A prayer of repentance is guaranteed to receive an immediate response if prayed with a sincere heart.

> ***"If we confess our sins, He is faithful and just to forgive us our sins and to cleanse us from all unrighteousness." (1 John 1:9, NKJV)***

No one is an island in the world. We live in a world where there are relatives, neighbors, job colleagues and friends. All these people have different emotional and spiritual make-ups. As a result, you are bound to encounter someone who may hurt you in one way or another. You are required to forgive. Forgiveness is an essential ingredient needed to open heaven's door in prayers.

> ***"And whenever you stand praying, if you have anything against anyone, forgive him, that your Father in heaven may also forgive you your trespasses. But if you do not forgive, neither will your Father in heaven forgive your trespasses." (Mark 11:25-26, NKJV)***

Remember you live in a world full of sin for the Bible says that all have sinned.

> ***"for all have sinned and fall short of the glory of God..." (Romans 3:23, NKJV)***

You need to forgive those that have sinned against you so that God will forgive your sins and you will appear sinless before Him as you offer your prayers at the midnight gate. If your sins are not forgiven, your prayer will never produce the desired result.

> ***"Now we know that God does not hear sinners..."***
> ***(John 9:31a, NKJV)***

The forgiveness of your sin is very critical so that they don't hinder your prayers. In Matthew chapter 6, Jesus taught the disciples how to pray. He ended up his teaching on prayer by pointing at this critical ingredient needed to get heaven's door opened and prayers answered. This ingredient is a forgiving spirit.

> ***"For if you forgive men when they sin against you, your heavenly Father will also forgive you."***
> ***(Matthew 6:14, NIV)***

Forgiveness is also of paramount importance to couples. Praying together for their family, marriage, finances etc, couples need to let any bitterness go between them by taking it to the Lord. This way they can forgive each other and then pray using the midnight gate.

Faith is another important ingredient if you must get the door of heaven opened.

> ***"And whatever you ask for in prayer, having faith and (really) believing, you will receive."***
> ***(Matthew 21:22, AV)***

Faith is not a leap into the dark. It is, believing the unchanging words of the Bible. For your prayers to open the door of heaven and produce your desired results, when you pray, you must have faith. You must trust God for what He has said in the Scripture. You must believe!

"Therefore I say to you, whatever things you ask when you pray, believe that you receive them, and you will have them." (Mark 11:24, NKJV)

A very important ingredient required to get the door of heaven opened when you prayer, is the ingredient of fasting. I call it a "weapon of incredible and precise accomplishment" in the act of praying for results.

"Fasting enhances the power and focus of prayer. It is very potent 'spiritual atomic bomb' that can be used in a prayer battle at the midnight gate".

Fasting is the preparation for the battle while prayer is the battle proper.

"No demon can withstand a midnight gate confrontation with all the elements in place and the ingredients coated with the potent weapon of fasting"

Fasting prepares you for victory against satanic confrontations. Jesus demonstrated this when he fasted for 40 days and was victorious over all the attacks of Satan.

"Then Jesus, being filled with the Holy Spirit, returned from the Jordan and was led by the Spirit into the wilderness, being tempted for forty days by the devil. And in those days He ate nothing…"
(Luke 4:1-2, NKJV)

In the book of Matthew, the disciples were confronted by a demon-possessed boy whom they could not heal.

> ***"And when they had come to the multitude, a man came to Him, kneeling down to Him and saying, 'Lord, have mercy on my son, for he is an epileptic and suffers severely; for he often falls into the fire and often into the water. So I brought him to Your disciples, but they could not cure him.'"***
>
> ***(Matthew 17:14-16, NKJV)***

The disciples have cast out demons in the past and healed the sick. This particular case was not an easy one for them. They must have wondered why they could not heal the boy. Something must be missing. When they had an opportunity, they decided to ask Jesus why they could not set the boy free.

> ***"Then the disciples came to Jesus privately and said, 'Why could we not cast it out?'***
>
> ***(Matthew 17:19, NKJV)***

Jesus revealed to them that a very important ingredient was needed for an effective result in this situation.

> ***"...However, this kind does not go out except by prayer and fasting"***
>
> ***(Matthew 17:21, NKJV)***

Jesus said "...this kind..." There are situations and circumstances that require heaven's door to open for you which may be in the same category as the one Jesus referred to as "...this kind..." You require the fasting ingredient in other to have the desired result. Adding fasting to your prayers at the midnight gate is not a way of manipulating God into doing what you desire. Rather, fasting is a powerful ingredient needed to force yourself to focus and rely on God as you seek Him at the midnight gate for the purpose of getting the door of heaven opened unto your prayers. Fasting is a 'spiritual atomic bomb' that can be added to your prayers at the midnight gate, given by the LORD to destroy the strongholds of evil and open the door of heaven for the manifestation of your desired results in prayer. There is power in the ingredient of fasting as it puts you in contact with an all powerful God. Yes, you can still go a certain distance in achieving some results at the midnight gate when you pray without fasting. But the most incredible and powerful blessings always go to those who together with other ingredients and elements as enumerated in previous chapters, add fasting to their prayer lives. Apostle Paul made it clear that fasting was an important ingredient in his prayer life as an Apostle and Minister of Christ.

> ***"…in fastings often…"***
>
> ***(2 Corinthians 11:27b, NKJV)***

Moses fasted for 80 days. Elijah fasted for 40 days. The greatest spiritual leaders of the 20th century and today who made and are making impacts for the Lord are all men and women of fasting. Such God's servants as Wesley, Finney, Bonnke, Cho, Annacondia and several others are all men of much fasting to the best of my knowledge. You need to make use of this powerful ingredient at the midnight gate. God, Himself exhorts His people to seek Him, utilizing this important ingredient.

> ***"Consecrate a fast, Call a sacred assembly; Gather the elders And all the inhabitants of the land Into the house of the LORD your God, And cry out to the LORD."***
>
> ***(Joel 1:14, NKJV)***

You can find different types of fast such as Esther fasts and others in numerous good Christian books on fasting to adopt a good kind of fasting method to add to your prayers at the midnight gate. You need the manifold presence of God in prayers to stop the devil as you pray to get the door of heaven opened.

Another powerful and important ingredient you need to open heaven's door as you pray is praise. Praise drives you into the realm of the supernatural and into the power of God as you seek Him in prayer. Paul and Silas have a good understanding of the secret of this ingredient to lift their hearts above their problems. They added it to their fervent prayer at the midnight gate while in the Philippi prison. You know the result. The use of praise by Paul and Silas at the midnight gate while they prayed provided God a channel for the manifestation and operation of His power in their difficult circumstance. According to Scriptures, God dwells in the atmosphere of praise.

> ***"But You are holy, enthroned in the praises of Israel." (Psalm 22:3, NKJV)***

This means that praise is a 'visa' which allows you to enter into the sacredness of God's glory and power. You need the powerful atmosphere of His presence and praise ushers you into it. God's presence repels the presence of the devil. This means that an atmosphere saturated with praises to God is disgusting and repugnant to the devil. Praise, therefore sends the enemy packing when you utilize it as an ingredient in praying at the midnight gate.

Chapter 9

Possess the Gates

Whosoever controls the gate influences the city!

There are physical gates and there are spiritual gates. The Bible made mention of different kinds of gates and the kinds of activities that take place there. Literarily, gates are points that permit the entrance or exit into a place. Gates are also points of transition that marks the end of a phase/era or the starting of another. Thus it is a point of transformation from one state to another. In view of these definitions, the midnight is a gate for it is the point of transition that marks the end of the night and the starting point of the morning. It therefore follows that your day has a gate. So also is your week, month, and year.

Let us look at the gates in the Old Testament times. According to Lawrence O. Richards in Encyclopedia of Bible Words, there are three images suggested by the role of city gates in Old Testament times.

The first is that of a controlled access and strongly fortified.

> ***"Then the men pursued them by the road to the Jordan, to the fords. And as soon as those who pursued them had gone out, they shut the gate."***
> ***(Joshua 2:7, NKJV)***

The second image is legal or governmental in character. The leaders of a city sat at the gates. There the elders or the king handed down judicial decisions.

> ***"Then the king arose and sat in the gate. And they told all the people, saying, "There is the king, sitting in the gate." So all the people came before the king. For everyone of Israel had fled to his tent." (2 Samuel 19:8, NKJV)***

The third image is that of business and social functions. It was at the city gates that business contracts were made and witnessed. Also markets were set up just outside the city gates.

> ***"And all who went out of the gate of his city heeded Hamor and Shechem his son; every male was circumcised, all who went out of the gate of his city." (Genesis 34:24, NKJV)***

According to Lawrence O. Richards, Old Testament prophets sometimes took their stand at this key social location to sternly announce God's messages.

> ***"Thus the LORD said to me: "Go and stand in the gate of the children of the people, by which the kings of Judah come in and by which they go out, and in all the gates of Jerusalem; and say to them, 'Hear the word of the LORD, you kings of Judah, and all Judah, and all the inhabitants of Jerusalem, who enter by these gates."***
>
> ***(Jeremiah 17:19-20, NKJV)***

Having seen what the Bible has to say about gates, you agree with me that there is a great need to possess the gate of your day, the gate of your week, the gate of your month, and the gate of your year. A lot of churches organize prayers by midnight of December 31 each year. Many people do not understand the symbolic nature and spiritual implication of these yearly services. However, in some churches, it is a time of entertainment while in others it is a time of serious intercession for the coming year. The spiritual implication of December 31 midnight service is that children of God should pray and take spiritual control of the affairs of the coming year, This can be achieved by gathering in God's house and praying at the midnight gate.

In December 2008, the Lord spoke to me that God's children in His church that I pastor in Mesquite, (Dallas), Texas, USA can take spiritual control of every month in 2009 by possessing the gates of each month of the year. In compliance to this, the church started a prayer program tagged "Possessing the Gate". We gather on the last day of every month and pray from 10pm to 1am after fasting on the last three days of the month. This prayer session is carried out irrespective of the day of the week that marks the last day of the month. There have been great and powerful testimonies following this monthly prayer exercise. During these possessing the gate prayers, we normally experience awesome manifestations of the presence of the Holy Ghost with people getting slain in the spirit, demons wailing and leaving people as well as powerful testimonies of healing. I normally post prayer points for each month on the church website at www.chapelofrevival.org or www.valegbudiwe.org. Please feel free to visit the web site, download the prayer points, follow the instructions and participate in the monthly "Possessing the Gate" prayers.

The midnight gate is a strategic entry location into a new day, week, month, or year. You need to stand in this important spiritual strategic location and release your spiritual arsenals through prayers against the devil. You need to turn your battle against the forces of hell at the midnight gate in other to open heaven's door and get the desired answers to your prayers. Possess the gates!

Chapter 10

21-Day Midnight Gate Prayers

The prayers given in this chapter are suggestions. You are free to adopt your own strategies and prayer points based on the revelations you have caught in this book and depending on your circumstances. I have designed the prayers as a guide to coach and encourage you to adopt a 21-day midnight gate prayer exercise.

Before you engage in this prayer exercise, ensure you are genuinely born-again. If you are not, you may go ahead and give your life to Jesus Christ now:

There are FOUR fundamental and basic Spiritual laws:

1. You are loved by God and He has a plan for your life: Irrespective of what you have done in the past, it does not matter how well or bad you think that you have been. God has prepared a special plan for your life that only you can fulfill. This is because you are very important to God.

2. Your own good deeds cannot earn you God's love: Christianity and Religion are fundamentally different. Religion teaches that it is through good works that one becomes right with God. However, the Bible says

> ***For by grace you have been saved through faith, and that not of yourselves; it is the gift of God, not***

of works, lest anyone should boast.
(Ephesians 2:8-9, NKJV)

3. Jesus Christ, the Son of God died for our sins: You cannot be good enough to please God on your own. No matter how you try you will always fall short because of your nature that causes you to sin. The Bible says

> ***Therefore, just as through one man sin entered the world, and death through sin, and thus death spread to all men, because all sinned—***
> ***(Romans 5:12, NKJV)***

God sent His son Jesus to die on the cross in place of sinful man. It is only through faith in Christ that your sins can be forgiven and you can gain righteousness with God.

4. It is only through faith in Jesus Christ that one can be saved: God has every right to decide what He will accept as the correct way to come to Him. He is the Creator of the universe. Fortunately God is also very kind and compassionate. He has provided a way for mankind to be forgiven and saved, and that way is through faith in Jesus Christ.

> ***Nor is there salvation in any other, for there is no other name under heaven given among men by which we must be saved."***
> ***(Acts 4:12, NKJV)***

Having read and assimilated these fundamental truths, confess your sins, repent and forsake them, then say this simple prayer:

"Almighty God, I know that I have sinned, and that no amount of good works could ever make up for that. I have realized that in my own power, I cannot help myself. I believe that You love me, and that You sent Your Son Jesus Christ to die for me. You alone can help me. Please forgive me of all my sins. I believe in my heart that Jesus Christ is the Son of God. I also confess with my mouth that He is my Lord and personal Savior. I now invite you dear Jesus to come into my heart and teach me how I should live. Thank You for loving me so much and for saving me. Grant me the grace to be faithful in my walk with You and also to be able to make Heaven in Jesus' name, Amen."

Now that you are saved, you can commence the 21-Day Midnight Gate prayers.

Suggested Tips

- One important thing you must have in mind is that you are not praying against any human being that is alive or dead. You are directing your prayers against spiritual entities that you may not even know or see.

  "For we do not wrestle against flesh and blood, but against principalities, against powers, against the rulers of the darkness of this age, against spiritual

hosts of wickedness in the heavenly places."

(Ephesians 6:12, NKJV)

- You can pray during the day but please do not miss to pray by midnight preferably between the hours by 12:00am and 03:00am. This is the midnight gate. Wage war against the devil at the midnight gate. The devil will lose the battle at the gate if you use the ingredients and follow the instructions and the guidance of the Holy Ghost. The gate is important to the devil because at the gate the hearts of men could be stolen. When he fought to overthrow David through his son, Absalom, the devil used the principle of contact at the gate to turn the hearts of the men of Israel.

"Now Absalom would rise early and stand beside the way to the gate." ***(2 Samuel 15:2a, NKJV)***

"In this manner Absalom acted toward all Israel who came to the king for judgment. So Absalom stole the hearts of the men of Israel."

(2 Samuel 15:6, NKJV)

When you pray is very important. Do not miss the midnight.

- Strive to adopt the principles enumerated in this book. Most of all use the ingredients. Repentance is paramount. It is very important to mention the sins you committed by name, one by one and sincerely forsake them and ask God for forgiveness. Receive His forgiveness by faith.

- ***"He who covers his sins will not prosper, but whoever confesses and forsakes them will have mercy." (Proverbs 28:13, NKJV)***

- Apart from adopting all the other ingredients if you desperately need a quick result to your prayers, add fasting to it. Fast for 21 days depending on your health condition. I suggest you adopt the method of Esther for the first three days. (The Esther type of fast involves staying 3 days without food or water). Ask the Holy Ghost for wisdom please.

- Study the Bible always especially during the 21 days. Discover the scriptures relevant to your prayer needs and convert them into prayer points. These will form your arsenals to launch prayer attacks.

- Start and close every prayer session with powerful praise and worship.

- Sow a 'seed of faith' to your church or an orphanage at the end of the 21 days

The sample prayers I have given here are divided into three segments. This means that you will use the same prayer points each day for the first week, another set of prayer points each day for the second and third week making all together 21 days.

Week 1 (1-7 days)

- Praise and Worship (Spend 15 minutes praising and worshipping God with your whole heart)

- Anoint yourself with oil (on the first day).
-
- ***"It shall come to pass in that day that his burden will be taken away from your shoulder, And his yoke from your neck, And the yoke will be destroyed because of the anointing oil "***

  (Isaiah 10:27, NKJV)

Confessions

Personalize these Scriptures and confess them aloud before you begin to pray aggressively.

- ***"And those who are Christ's have crucified the flesh with its passions and desires."***
(Galatians 5:24, NKJV)

- ***Christ has redeemed us from the curse of the law, having become a curse for us (for it is written, "Cursed is everyone who hangs on a tree"), that the blessing of Abraham might come upon the Gentiles in Christ Jesus, that we might receive the promise of the Spirit through faith.***
(Galatians 3:13-14, NKJV)

- ***Therefore if anyone cleanses himself from the latter, he will be a vessel for honor, sanctified and useful for the Master, prepared for every good work.*** ***(2 Timothy 2:21, NKJV)***

Prayer Points

1. I use the power in the Blood of Jesus Christ to sanctify the environment of this locality in Jesus name.

2. I use the Blood of Jesus Christ to set a standard against any evil spiritual opposition to my prayers in Jesus name.

3. I dismantle spiritually, every evil altar working against my prayers and destiny in this environment. I speak destruction to all the evil chief priests attached to these altars in Jesus name.

4. O Lord, let your warring angels arise and cleanse my environment with your fire in Jesus name.

5. Fire of God, saturate my environment and bring forth testimonies as I pray in Jesus name.

6. I command every spiritual pipe in me to receive cleansing as I declare today that the fire on my prayer altar will never go down in Jesus name.

7. O Lord, send your axe of fire to the foundation of my life and destroy every evil plantation and inherited deposits in Jesus name.

8. I break loose from all evil inherited covenants and curses in Jesus name.

9. I spiritually vomit every evil consumption that I have been fed as a child or in my dreams. Fire of the Holy

Ghost, burn within me and destroy them in Jesus name.

10. I command to be opened, all doors of blessings shut against me as a result of evil associations or ancestral evil foundations in Jesus name.

11. I command the fire of the Holy Ghost to roast all forces of inheritance and obstacles in my prayer life and destiny. Let all their powers be paralyzed in Jesus name.

12. I break loose from the control and manipulation of all evil gates as I spiritually take hold of the gates of my destiny in Jesus name.

13. I break and destroy every curse and covenant which empowers witchcraft and familiar spirits to operate in my life in Jesus name.

14. Every curse of profitless hard work and slow progress in my life, I command you to be broken in Jesus name.

15. I use the Blood of Jesus to neutralize all satanic and negative arrangements against me within the constellations as I speak to the sun, moon, and stars to begin to favor me in Jesus name.

16. I shake off every season of frustration and failure; and also dismantle every evil calendar for my life in Jesus name.

17. I dismantle any siege of the enemy against me and I command any power assigned to cause accidents in my

life to scatter. I declare that I will not die untimely in Jesus name.

18. All handwriting of ordinances programmed into the heavens against me, I use the Blood of Jesus Christ to wipe you out in Jesus name.

19. As I take hold of the gate of my life, I declare that this is my season of blessings for the spirit of favor, might and power shall come upon me in Jesus name

20. O LORD, anoint me with oil of gladness above my fellows as I declare that from now onwards, my ear shall hear good news only and I shall not hear the voice of the enemy in Jesus name.

21. Begin to prophesy upon your life and command the gate of the day, week, month, or year to open by fire and release your blessings in Jesus name.

Week 2 (8-14 days)

- Praise and Worship (Spend 15 minutes praising and worshipping God with your whole heart)
- Anoint yourself with oil (On the 8th Day)

Confessions

Personalize these Scriptures and confess them aloud before you begin to pray aggressively

- ***"The LORD will cause your enemies who rise against you to be defeated before your face; they*** *shall come out against you one way and flee before you seven ways."* *(Deuteronomy 28:7, NKJV)*

- *Behold, I give you the authority to trample on serpents and scorpions, and over all the power of the enemy, and nothing shall by any means hurt you.* *(Luke 10:13, NKJV)*

-

- *I will be glad and rejoice in Your mercy for You have considered my trouble; You have known my soul in adversities* *(Psalm 31:7, NKJV)*

- *If My people who are called by My name will humble themselves, and pray and seek My face, and turn from their wicked ways, then I will hear from heaven, and will forgive their sin and heal their land. Now My eyes will be open and My ears attentive to prayer made in this place.*
(2 Chronicles 7:14-15, NKJV)

-

- *Oh, that You would rend the heavens! That You would come down! That the mountains might shake at Your presence— As fire burns brushwood, As fire causes water to boil— To make Your name known to Your adversaries, That the nations may tremble at Your presence!*
(Isaiah 64:1-2, NKJV)

Prayer Points

(Repeat Prayer Points 1-5 of Week 1)

1. I release my soul from every evil cage and I ask the ministering angels of God to search the land of the living and dead, including the dream world and covens of Satan and liberate my soul in Jesus name.

2. I pull down every intimidating spirit working against my blessings and divine upliftment in Jesus name.

3. O LORD, let your military angels begin to attack my enemies, my attackers, my pursuers and destroyers in Jesus name.

4. I send the sword of God against every spiritual wickedness in the heavenlies militating against my star. I frustrate your activities in Jesus name.

5. I send thunder, lightning, hail stones and arrows of God against any evil queen or prince in the air, land or water that is working against my life in Jesus name.

6. I use the Blood of Jesus Christ to wipe away any evidence brought against me by wicked spirits to stop my blessings in Jesus name.

7. Every power aborting the purposes of God for my life, I speak destruction to you now in Jesus name.

8. O Lord, break off the spirit and life behind hardship and problems in my life in Jesus name.

9. I command the fire of the Holy Ghost to burn to ashes every satanic power tampering with my future and divine destiny in Jesus name.

10. Every satanic prison, store house, bank and warehouse in the water, air, or land harboring my blessings, let the thunder of God smash you open to release my divine blessings in Jesus name.

11. Every evil midnight incantations and enchantments against me backfire in the name of Jesus.

12. Any invisible evil chain or chord tying my hands and legs break down now in Jesus name.

13. All evil congregations of household wickedness, marine powers, ancestral powers, and rulers of darkness, I pronounce and decree destruction to every roadblock you have placed against the channel of my blessings in Jesus name.

14. Let the fire of the Holy Ghost begin to destroy all monitoring devices, the devil and his agents are using to monitor my progress and advancement in Jesus name.

15. Every evil power or person monitoring my life at the midnight hour, let the shining light of God blind you in Jesus name.

16. I destroy the existence in my life of all producers and providers of sickness, poverty, marital crisis, fear, bad luck and confusion in Jesus name

17. Every evil power manipulating the elements of nature and the land where I live to fight me and stop my blessing, receive angelic attack and be scattered in Jesus name.

18. O Lord, bring honey out of the rock for me in Jesus name.

19. Every dormant talent in me, come forth now and propel me for global recognition and prosperity in Jesus name.

20. Any evil power using the dust and sand of the earth to manipulate my business, marriage, careers, and prosperity, receive God's judgment by fire as I declare that I will be blessed all-round in this land for it is written: Wherever the sole of my feet shall tread upon is given to me for a possession in Jesus name.

21. Begin to prophesy upon your life and thank God for answered prayers.

Week 3 (15-21 days)

- Praise and Worship (Spend 15 minutes praising and worshipping God with your whole heart)

- Anoint yourself with oil (on the 15th day).

Confessions

Personalize these Scriptures and confess them aloud before you begin to pray aggressively

- *Every good gift and every perfect gift is from above, and comes down from the Father of lights, with whom there is no variation or shadow of turning.* *(James 1:17, NKJV)*
-
- *"And to the angel of the church in Philadelphia write, 'These things says He who is holy, He who is true, "He who has the key of David, He who opens and no one shuts, and shuts and no one opens": "I know your works. See, I have set before you an open door, and no one can shut it; for you have a little strength, have kept My word, and have not denied My name.* *(Revelation 3:7-8, NKJV)*

- *The LORD is your keeper; The LORD is your shade at your right hand. The sun shall not strike you by day Nor the moon by nigh*
- *(Psalm 121:5-6, NKJV)*
-
- *I will give you the treasures of darkness, And hidden riches of secret places, That you may know that I, the LORD, Who call you by your name, Am the God of Israel.* *(Isaiah 45:3, NKJV)*

Prayer Points

(Repeat Prayer Points 1-5 of Week 1)

1. O Lord, let my season of miracles, testimonies, and divine intervention appear in Jesus name.

2. Let the covenant blessings of Abraham begin to manifest in my life in Jesus name.

3. I declare that I shall be the head and not the tail for as from today, in the mighty name of Jesus, I am blessed in my going out and in my coming in.

4. My body is the temple of the Holy Ghost therefore sickness and afflictions cannot thrive in me for I declare that no weapon formed against me shall prosper in Jesus name.

5. The stripes of Jesus heal me of every infirmity as I call upon Jehovah Rophe to rearrange my genetic code to reject every satanic disease in Jesus name.

6. I prophesy and release creative miracles of God into every area of my life in Jesus name.

7. Arise, O LORD, scatter and destroy all evil gatekeepers assigned against my life in Jesus name.

8. The Lord has surrounded me with favor for He takes delight in my prosperity; therefore, I call all my divine helpers to begin to locate me in Jesus name.

9. O LORD, give me anointed and intelligent ideas that will lead me to new paths of blessing in Jesus name.

10. O LORD, perfect all things that concern me and let all my disappointments of previous years become divine appointments in Jesus name.

11. Almighty God, guide and direct me to rectify all problems I have with my life, marriage, career spiritually and materially in Jesus name.

12. I refuse to walk in the counsel of the ungodly, stand in the path of sinners nor sit in the seat of the scornful but my delight is in God's word therefore whatever I do shall prosper in Jesus name.

13. I reject debt, lack, insufficiency and famine in my life in Jesus name.

14. I nullify and condemn every negative word and pronouncement spoken against my success by myself or other people in Jesus name.

15. Holy Ghost, teach me to avoid unfriendly friends or associates and unprofitable transactions in Jesus name.

16. I break all curses of failure at the edge of miracle as I bind the spirit of negative destiny in every area of my life in Jesus name.

17. Every garment of shame, filthiness, dishonor, spiritual and material laziness, depression and poverty on me, be roasted in Jesus name.

18. From this day, I cast out of my life, every spirit of delay, hindrance, slavery, and hardship in Jesus name.

19. I withdraw my breakthroughs, blessings, prosperity, and glory from any evil altar in Jesus name.

20. Begin to prophetically call the things you desire by name and command them to answer and manifest in Jesus name.

21. Thank God for answered prayers and spend at least 15 minutes in thanksgiving, praise, and worship.

References

1. Elisha Goodman, "Passion Prayer of Jesus the Christ". USA: Xilbris Corporation, 2004
2. Olukoya, D.K., "Prayer Rain", Lagos: MFM Press 1999
3. Lawrence O. Richards, "Encyclopedia of Bible Words", Michigan: Zondervan 1991
4. Peter Horrobin, "Healing through Deliverance 2", England: Sovereign World 1995.

Praise Reports

If you carried out the 21-Day Midnight Gate prayers and has a praise report you would love to share with the Author, you may contact him at:

Val Egbudiwe World Outreach,
1427 Colborne Drive,
Mesquite, Texas 75149, USA.
Web Site: www.valegbudiwe.org
E-Mail: vewoutreach@aol.com
Tel: 1-972-288 2882 OR 1-214-673 8030

FOR SPEAKING ENGAGEMENTS, CONTACT THE AUTHOR USING THE INFORMATION ABOVE.

About Val Egbudiwe

Val Egbudiwe is an international Missionary/Revival Evangelist and Pastor. A Bachelor of Science graduate of the University of Nigeria, Nsukka, Theology trained alumnus of Faith Bible College and Seminary, Lagos, Nigeria and a CPE trained Chaplain (Pastoral Care Department, Methodist Health Systems, Dallas, Texas, USA). He is currently a graduate student of Practical Theology at the Southwestern Assemblies of God University, Waxahachie, Texas, USA.

Val Egbudiwe was called of God with a unique mandate and anointing to deliver God's people from the bondage of sin, Satan and poverty. God's presence is always manifested as God confirms His Word with signs and wonders when he preaches the Word. A very powerful, vibrant and eloquent preacher, the ministry of Val Egbudiwe is in high demand in many parts of the world. While in Nigeria, Africa, he basically preached in crusades winning souls in thousands especially within the rural areas and preaching revival in churches. The service of God has taken him to many nations of Africa. He has also ministered at the famous Trinity Broadcasting Network (TBN) Television studio watched by millions of people in South Africa as well as done extensive evangelistic work in Europe including the former communist country, Romania.

With a great insight into spiritual warfare, Val Egbudiwe also operates in the miraculous as his ministry is always accompanied with demonstration of the power of the Holy Ghost to save, heal and set the captives free. He is licensed by the United Christian Church and Ministerial Association, Cleveland, Tennessee, USA and ordained by Harvests Fields Ministries, MO, USA and the Redeemed Christian Church of God, North America. He is the Founder of Val Egbudiwe World Outreach Incorporated, an international Non-Profit Evangelistic and Apostolic Organization based in Dallas, Texas. He is also currently the Pastor of Chapel of Revival and Miracles Church, a parish of The Redeemed Christian Church of God based in Mesquite, (Dallas), Texas and planted by him.

He has ministered in several churches in many states in the US bringing revivals as God has used him to turn many to Christ in these churches. Val Egbudiwe is married to his wife and Ministry supporter, Edith and they are blessed with three girls and one boy.

Breinigsville, PA USA
28 October 2009
226668BV00002B/2/P